# *the art of*
# real food

Seasonal Recipes for Every Week of the Year

Real Dirt ❧ Real Food ❧ Real Health

# *the art of*
# real food

### Seasonal Recipes for Every Week of the Year

Joanne Neft and Laura Kenny

First Edition


Copyright 2012 by Joanne Neft and Laura Kenny
Photography by Keith Sutter
Paintings by Paula Amerine
Ceramics by Anthony Maki Gill

Published by In Season Publishing Company
P. O. Box 753
Newcastle, CA 95658


www.theartofrealfood.com


Printed in the USA


Library of Congress Cataloging-in-Publication Data
Neft, Joanne and Kenny, Laura
The Art of Real Food cookbook/Joanne Neft and Laura Kenny; Photography by Keith Sutter;
Paintings by Paula Amerine; Ceramics by Anthony Maki Gill
ISBN- 978-0-984-95860-3


1. Farmers Market – California. 2. Cookery. 3. Neft, Joanne and Kenny, Laura.

For the farmers who nourish our bodies
and the artists who stretch our minds

# Food Can Change Your Life

*N*ot so long ago, my partner and I found ourselves the heaviest we'd ever been. We were taking pills for high blood pressure and for high cholesterol. We had heartburn, couldn't sleep and were completely addicted to sugar and processed foods.

I realized just what a dangerous game we were playing after flying out to see his newest musical opening. We'd been apart about a month, and I was shocked when I saw him. He'd gained at least five pounds, as had I. My heart sank for both of us. When the show closed, he came home to a partner who had had enough. Deep down, I knew he had, too.

During this time, some friends were starting their second class on nutrition and healthy eating. We signed up, even though we thought we already knew a lot about food and health. We sat in class every Wednesday night for a solid month, and learned about real food, about healthy food, about food from the farmers market.

Five days into the process I had an epiphany. I looked at my partner, and said incredulously, "I don't have any food cravings." Normally I am obsessed about the next meal, about what we are going to eat and when. I suddenly realized I hadn't been buying candy bars while filling up the gas tank, and I hadn't been eating cookies as a mid-afternoon snack. I chose water instead.

We cleaned out our pantry, began planning menus and discovered the joys of shopping at farmers markets. I never knew mandarin oranges were so delicious. Fresh, farm-grown meat tasted like nothing we'd ever had before, even though we've eaten at world-class restaurants across the country. We saw vegetables of every color imaginable. And we learned how to prepare simple, clean foods to make meals that satisfied us and helped us rebuild our health quickly and naturally. And along the way we watched at least seven inspiring documentaries on the farm-to-table movement and healthy eating.

Today we are 65 pounds lighter and off all but one medication, which we believe we will be able to quit taking soon. No more allergy pills. No more heartburn. Deep, restful nights of sleep are back. And it's all because of the food we eat and the food we do not.

I'm proud to be part of this movement. We're fortunate to have leaders like Joanne Neft and Laura Kenny sharing their knowledge and love of healthy food and of farmers markets. They give us all the chance to have a fuller, richer, healthier life.

Joe Zaniker, President, Graphic Focus
www.graphic-focus.com

# Sponsors

**Community 1st Bank**

**Newcastle Produce**

**Placer Community Foundation**

Ellen MacInnes, Senior Vice President, Morgan Stanley Smith Barney
Eisley Nursery
Cooking Gallery
Foothill Farmers Market
Auburn Drug

Bushnell Gardens Nursery

Blue Goose Produce
Recology
Placer Breast Cancer Endowment
Maki Heating and Air Conditioning, Inc.
Windeshausen Family
Mandarin Valley Candles
Skyridge Elementary School

Highland Orchard Inc.
Side Hill Citrus
Jordan Family Farms
Miller Citrus Grove

# Table of Contents

Acknowledgements....................................12

Foreword................................................13

Introduction ..........................................14

Tips from the Chef ..................................17

January 1: Meyer Lemons..........................19

January 8: Nuts ......................................27

January 15: Broccoli ................................33

January 22: Root Vegetables....................39

January 29: Cauliflower ...........................45


February 5: Fennel ..................................49

February 12: Endive................................55

February 19: Oranges..............................61

February 26: Cabbage.............................65


March 5: Beets ......................................71

March 12: Potatoes ................................75

March 19: Lettuce ..................................81

March 26: Mushrooms ............................85

April 2: Grains ......................................89

April 9: Carrots......................................93

April 16: Eggs .......................................99

April 23: Herbs .....................................105

April 30: Red Chard and Rhubarb.............111


May 7: Onions .......................................117

May 14: Strawberries .............................123

May 21: Blueberries ...............................127

May 28: Cherries ...................................133


June 4: Dried Beans ...............................139

June 11: Arugula ...................................143

June 18: Summer Squash.........................149

June 25: Nectarines ...............................153

# Table of Contents

July 2: Figs ...................................... 159

July 9: Cucumbers .......................... 165

July 16: Tomatoes ........................... 171

July 23: Peaches ............................. 177

July 30: Corn .................................. 183


August 6: Blackberries ..................... 187

August 13: Pink-Eyed Peas ............... 195

August 20: Green Beans ................... 199

August 27: Roma Tomatoes .............. 203


September 3: Melons ....................... 207

September 10: Grapes ..................... 211

September 17: Green Tomatoes, Cherry

    Tomatoes & Tomatillos .............. 217

September 24: Peppers .................... 223

October 1: Apples ........................... 227

October 8: Persimmons .................... 233

October 15: Eggplant ...................... 239

October 22: Pears ........................... 245

October 29: Winter Squash .............. 251


November 5: Celery ......................... 257

November 12: Honey ....................... 261

November 19: Spinach ..................... 265

November 26: Kale .......................... 269


December 3: Garlic .......................... 273

December 10: Citrus Medley ............ 279

December 17: Mandarins .................. 283

December 24: Sweet Potatoes .......... 287

December 31: Pomegranates ............ 291

# Acknowledgements

It takes more than two people to create a cookbook. The initial concept is only the beginning. More than a few friends and associates guided us and provided feedback, encouragement and support.

This book is all about art: the art of preparing, presenting, and writing about food. Paula Amerine enthusiastically focused on produce and illustrated it; Anthony Maki Gill made unique ceramic serving pieces; Keith Sutter captured the recipes in photographs. Several photos were taken on utilitarian platters and bowls made by gifted ceramist Dick Ketelle.

Always there when we needed her, Debbie Dutra was "Debbie on the spot" throughout the process. Her ever-present sense of humor pulled us through a few rough spots. Betsy Dell and Niesha Lofing brought their meaningful story-telling skills and wrote them down. And writer Pat Rubin was copy editor/organization manager supreme.

Michele Tuggle of Mprint Studios performed her magic designing the book, and Michele Parry furnished a workable website at just the right time. It's important to mention Joe Zaniker, president of Graphic Focus, who doggedly remained on task to find a printer in the United States to honor our request to print this cookbook on American soil.

Over a period of 15 months a host of growers and ranchers cheered us on as we purchased all the recipe ingredients. Particularly helpful were Carol Arnold, market manager, and Dan Macon, lamb purveyor, at local farmers markets.

Finally, bouquets to Jerry Burns for carrying more bundles of produce than he ever dreamed possible, for tasting all the recipes, and for sharing chocolate treats and armloads of flower arrangements.

*Joanne Neft*

# Foreword

When someone asks whether I enjoy cooking, I answer "yes" because I genuinely do. As a newlywed and young mother, my "yes" culminated in a lively exchange of recipes and favorite cookbook titles. By the time my kids were in junior high, friends were also asking "Do you cook often?" And I'd reply, "Not anymore." No one asked why. We'd simply bemoan how busy we were with kids, carpools and committees.

But I wasn't too busy, and I certainly hadn't quit feeding my family. I simply rarely cooked. What had been a daily delight had become a hobby, something I did when I could, like playing tennis or scrapbooking. Had life changed so much? Honestly, it had not. Getting kids to soccer wasn't more tiring than toddlers; grass stains weren't harder to remove than baby urp.

What changed was our attitude toward instant meals. Somewhere between the time when my kids were little and today society gentrified mass prepared food. Ready-made dinners appeared on grocery store fresh food shelves. We stopped cooking because it wasn't necessary. We could feed our families without actually buying, preparing and cooking the ingredients that went into a recipe. And I forgot I love to cook.

Then I met Joanne Neft and Chef Laura Kenny. Their book, *Placer County Real Food from Farmers Markets: Recipes and Menus for Every Week of the Year*, gave me a reason to cook again. It wasn't the beautiful photos, or the recipes I could savor by simply reading. No, I had plenty of cookbooks that tickled my taste buds. The reason was much simpler: Joanne and Laura reminded me why we eat. And I remembered why I love to cook.

Learning to think locally and seasonally lifted my food tin ennui, gave me new pleasure in shopping, and restored pride in what I put on the table. The change has affected my whole family. Together, we've reconnected with the food on our plates. Dinner is no longer perfunctory. We sit. We enjoy our food and each other. And, for the first time in many years, the blessing we speak over the meal has meaning.

I'm honored to introduce Joanne Neft and Laura Kenny's newest collaboration, *The Art of Real Food*. I want to be one of the first to say thank you for the all day cook-a-thons that made the book possible. Thank you for your passion for real food, and for the zeal with which you share it.

Of course, there are many whose lives you've already changed for the better. To those who will meet Joanne and Laura for the first time inside these pages, let me simply say prepare to have the cooking fire re-lit within you.

Betsy Dell, Mom

# Introduction

When Laura Kenny and I completed *Placer County Real Food from Farmers Markets: Recipes and Menus for Every Week of the Year,* we had no intention of writing another cookbook. After all, we'd achieved our purpose, which was to expose people to the seasonal treasures of the farmers market by identifying lesser known fruits and vegetables and providing ways to prepare them. As we put our pens down and pots away, we had no idea our cookbook would do something much more important: it would foster a grassroots dialogue about food.

Why do we call it grassroots? It's because the people talking include your sister, your friend's mother, and your neighbor. And given the nation's increasing dependence on experts to tell us what to eat, who is talking – we, the people – is especially significant.

You see, the trouble with experts is they don't often agree. Just as one will vilify all fats, another will laud

their benefits, but shun carbohydrates. At best, these contradictions are confusing. At worst, they lead to decisions that are equally contradictory.

As author Michael Pollan noted in a 2007 *New York Times Magazine* piece, we've been taught to eat nutrients instead of food. The result is we're ok with serving breakfast cereals that taste like candy because they're fortified, and we'll drink juice from the bark of an obscure tree that only grows in the darkest reaches of Peru because it allegedly has a phytonutrient we can't pronounce said to magically prevent every disease known to man.

In such a climate the fact that regular people are talking about food – real food, born from soil and raised lovingly by a genuine farmer – means we're realizing we don't need experts or magic to manage our diets.

Enter the farmers market. The beauty of the farmers market is you needn't be a brain surgeon to feed yourself or your family. The latest arguments for or against fats, carbohydrates and sugars can be ignored because the foods available there are hormone and pesticide free. They haven't been irradiated, waxed or otherwise preserved for shipping. The vibrant colors and fresh smells that emblazon your senses weren't created or enhanced in a laboratory. It's just food. Real food.

The pleasure of the farmers market goes beyond the food it offers. It's about the community it fosters. It's a place where you build relationships with and respect for the people who grow your food. That relationship is critical to ensuring nature isn't programmed out of our lives.

Connecting food both to soil and toil is fundamental to making healthy eating choices. It's why this cookbook's cover features radishes freshly picked from breathing, composting dirt, and the cover of our first cookbook featured a farmer working in the field. We firmly believe the labor of the farmer brings us closer to our food as surely as the labor involved in manufacturing food takes us away from it.

What's thrilling is we're hearing these truths and realizations from people throughout the country. People email us; they stop us in the street, at the farmers market, at the grocery store. It's humbling and exciting to hear them say "You changed my life," and to witness their confidence in the food they're buying and preparing. It's inspiring to know we helped teach them how to nourish their bodies and we strengthened their connection to real food.

Their confidence runs deep, and it's fostered by knowledge that the only rule they need follow doesn't come from an expert. It comes from nature and from knowing why they no longer need rules. They've experienced the difference a diet of real food makes in relation to their health, energy levels, ability to concentrate, mood and appearance. They have come to believe, as we do, that you are what you eat.

As we listened to the stories, we came to understand our work wasn't done. The result is this, our latest cookbook. It's our hope these recipes and stories will continue the dialogue that's already begun, and hopefully will never end.

*Joanne Neft*

*I arise in the morning torn between a desire to save the world and a desire to savor the world. That makes it hard to plan the day.*
*—E. B. White*

Place a bouquet of flowers
on the table and everything
will taste twice as good.
—Michael Pollan

# Tips From The Chef

*By Laura Kenny*

*I*'d like to invite myself into your kitchen to offer a few tips. Promise, I won't be in the way, but I think these hints and bits of advice will make cooking fun and delicious.

❧ Think about leftovers and what to do with them before you prepare a meal. When we start with exceptional ingredients and prepare exceptional meals, it stands to reason we can have exceptional leftover creations. Making salmon? Buy extra for salmon cakes for the next meal. Leftover mashed potatoes? Check out our Stacked Potato and Placer Sweet Onion recipe (May 7). Other recipes, like Mushroom Arancini (March 26) and Halibut Croquettes (Sept. 10), are great ways to use leftovers. Either way, keep those leftovers; get creative and use them to build another meal.

❧ Many recipes call for making a reduction. We ask you to take a cup of mandarin juice, for example, and slowly cook it until there's only a quarter cup left. Why? A reduction is a way to concentrate a flavor. When reducing vinegars and juices, the best method is slow and easy to prevent burning.

❧ Although I love cast iron – heavy-bottomed, even heating and searing results – it's not ideal for everything. Acidic items such as tomato sauces and fruits are better in stainless steel.

❧ We're constantly asked which oils and salts we prefer in our recipes. We're fortunate to have some wonderful companies in our area that produce quality olive oil. Look at your farmers market for similar companies, or ask around about what's available in your area. As a rule of thumb, we use grapeseed oil for searing and sautéing, and a combination of butter and olive oil for cooking vegetables, and finally, extra virgin olive oil to finish dishes. We love salt, and use kosher salt and fine sea salt for general cooking. Specialized salts with their larger grains make a nice garnish and add a bit of crunch and flavor.

❧ Everything is good in moderation is our code, and this includes rich cheeses, cream sauces and chocolate, all of which we refer to as "love." Add extra love to special occasion dishes, but not as an everyday occurrence.

❧ I'll say again the kitchen is a better place when you have sharp knives. This can make a difference in your final product and the amount of prep time.

❧ A good thermometer can save your dinner. Grass fed meats cook differently than commercial meats, and it's nice to know when you're about to turn your beautiful medium rare roast into jerky. Our favorite digital thermometer is made by Thermoworks; it's pricey, but worth every penny.

*There are painters who transform the sun to a yellow spot, but there are others who with the help of their art and their intelligence transform a yellow spot into the sun.*
          —Pablo Picasso

*january 1*

# Meyer Lemons

Salmon Cakes with Meyer Lemon Relish

Meyer Lemon Sour Pudding

Meyer Lemon Shaum Torte

Double Lemon Cake

Angel Food Cake with Meyer Lemon Sabayon Sauce

When recipes call for lemons, we use Meyer lemons, *Citrus x meyeri*. Reasonably hardy and well suited to mild winter climates, the Meyer lemon is native to China and thought to be a cross between a lemon and either a mandarin or a common orange.

The trees are vigorous, fast growers, and reach 6 to 10 feet at maturity. The fruit is rounder than other lemons; the thin, fragrant skin is deep yellow with a slight orange tint when ripe. The leaves are dark shiny green; the heavenly scented flowers are white with a purple base. Meyer lemons are sweeter and less acidic than Lisbon or Eureka varieties commonly found in grocery stores. They're perfect for zest.

Our Meyer lemon trees provide fresh fruit most of the year. We juice the lemons, and freeze the juice in ½ cup or 1 cup containers so we always have Meyer lemon juice for recipes no matter what time of year we want to make them.

# Meyer Lemons

## Salmon Cakes with Meyer Lemon Relish

Makes 6 to 8 cakes

1½ pounds salmon, cooked and shredded
3 stalks celery, diced
3 scallions, diced
1 tablespoon parsley, chopped
Salt and pepper to taste
1 egg, beaten
¾ cup panko breadcrumbs
2 tablespoons grapeseed oil

In a large bowl, combine salmon, celery, scallions and parsley. Season lightly with salt and pepper. Add egg and breadcrumbs, and stir to combine. Form into 2-ounce balls, squeezing them so they hold together, then into flat disks.
Heat oil in a large sauté pan, and sear cakes on both sides until golden brown, about 90 seconds. Serve warm with Meyer lemon relish.

### Meyer Lemon Relish

3 Meyer lemons, segmented
1 tablespoon olive oil
2 teaspoons capers, rinsed
Salt and pepper to taste

Combine lemon segments, olive oil and capers in a small bowl, and season to taste with salt and pepper. Serve with salmon cakes.

Citrus sections versus segments (also called supremes): Some recipes call for sections, others for segments. The difference is in the pith: a section has it and a segment does not.

When recipes call for sections, you simply peel the lemon or orange, and break it into slices, or pieces.

To make segments, cut off the ends of the citrus fruit, and then cut away the rind and the pith. Carefully cut each segment, avoiding the pith in between. It's a little time consuming, but dresses up your dish a little more. If you work over a bowl, you can save the juice to use later.

# Meyer Lemon Sour Pudding

Serves 6

*Thanks to Deanna Marsh for this recipe.*

Preheat oven to 350°F.

2 tablespoons flour

1 cup sugar

¼ teaspoon salt

3 tablespoons butter, softened

3 eggs, separated, yolks beaten, whites whipped until stiff

⅔ cup Meyer lemon juice

1 tablespoon Meyer lemon zest

1 cup milk

1 cup whipping cream, whipped

Shaved chocolate, for garnish

Sift flour, sugar and salt in a bowl. Add softened butter and mix together. Add beaten yolks, lemon juice, lemon zest and milk. Fold in stiffly beaten egg whites.

Bake in a buttered 2-quart soufflé dish (casserole dish) set in a pan of hot water 50 to 60 minutes.

When done, the soufflé will have a lightly browned, cake-like top with lemon pudding on the bottom.

Serve with a dollop of whipped cream and shaved chocolate.

Instead of baking in a soufflé dish, use individual ramekins or small Mason preserve jars. Bake 25 to 35 minutes.

---

Deanna Marsh invited me to lunch in the early spring and finished the meal with her grandmother's Meyer lemon sour pudding. The pudding surprised my palate. The taste begins with a tangy flavor, the texture wakes up the tongue, and the combination of flavors finishes the experience. It's one of my favorite recipes.

This pudding makes nice individual portions or can be spooned from the casserole dish into small dessert bowls at the table.

# Meyer Lemon Shaum Torte

Serves 8

Preheat oven to 275°F.

4 large farm fresh eggs, separated
½ teaspoon cream of tartar
1½ cups sugar
⅓ cup Meyer lemon juice
1 tablespoon Meyer lemon zest
1 cup whipping cream

Make a meringue by beating egg whites until bubbly; add cream of tartar. Continue to beat until slightly firm. Gradually add 1 cup sugar. Beat until stiff and glossy. Spread meringue in a well buttered 9-inch glass pie pan.

Bake 20 minutes. Increase temperature to 300°F and bake 40 minutes. Set aside to cool.

To make filling, beat egg yolks until lemon colored. Add remaining ½ cup sugar, lemon juice and zest. Cook in a double boiler until thick, stirring constantly. Cool slightly.

Whip cream until firm. Fold egg yolk mixture gently into cream. Spread over cooled meringue. Best refrigerated 24 hours before serving.

Top each piece of torte with a heaping teaspoon of raspberry or blackberry sauce or candied lemon rind.

# Double Lemon Cake

Serves 10 to 12

Preheat oven to 350°F.

3 cups cake flour
1 teaspoon baking soda
½ teaspoon salt
6 eggs, room temperature, separated
2 cups plus 1 teaspoon sugar
1 cup butter, room temperature
1 tablespoon lemon zest
3 tablespoons lemon juice
1 cup Greek yogurt

Sift flour, baking soda and salt together. Set aside.

In a mixing bowl, beat egg whites until soft peaks form. Slowly add ½ cup sugar and continue beating until stiff peaks form. Set aside.

In another bowl, cream butter, 1½ cups sugar, egg yolks, lemon zest and lemon juice until fluffy. Add yogurt to egg yolk mixture. Add flour to egg yolk mixture. Gently fold in egg whites. Generously butter a 10-inch Bundt-style pan, and lightly sprinkle 1 teaspoon white sugar into pan (sugar helps cake release easier from pan). Pour batter into pan.

Bake 50 to 60 minutes, until cake is set. Remove from oven and rest 10 minutes. Turn cake onto a wire rack to cool.

Serve plain, or with chocolate or lemon sauce.

*Don't eat anything your great-grandmother wouldn't recognize as food.* –Michael Pollan

⤳ I eat yogurt every day. I make sure my regular diet also includes other fermented foods because they are good for my health. When buying fermented foods, look for key words and phrases such as "live" and "active cultures" on yogurt, and the word "raw" on fermented vegetables (sauerkraut and pickles).

# Meyer Lemons

## Angel Food Cake with Meyer Lemon Sabayon Sauce

Serves 10 to 12

Preheat oven to 350°F.

1 cup cake flour
1½ cups sugar
½ teaspoon salt
1½ cups free-range egg whites (about 12 large eggs), room temperature
1 teaspoon cream of tartar
2 tablespoons Meyer lemon juice
⅓ cup Meyer lemon zest
Shaved chocolate for garnish

Sift flour, then measure, and place in a bowl. Add ½ cup sugar and salt to flour and sift twice more. Set aside.

Beat egg whites in a large, clean bowl. When whites are foamy, add cream of tartar and 1 tablespoon lemon juice. When bubbles are uniform, add remaining cup of sugar a few tablespoons at a time. Beat whites until they form stiff peaks (when you lift the beaters a peak will form and hold) and sugar is dissolved.

Fold in the flour with a clean rubber spatula, using a down-the-side-and-up-through-the-batter motion. Do not over mix.

Fold in the lemon zest and remaining Meyer lemon juice.

When mixture is thoroughly combined, turn into a very clean grease-free 10-inch tube pan.

Bake 50 minutes. Test for doneness by pressing lightly in center of cake; if it springs back, cake is done. Remove from oven and invert pan until cake is cool.

The cake must be raised an inch or more above the counter during cooling process. An easy way to do this is to invert the cake pan over a wine-type bottle.

When cool, remove cake by running a serrated knife around edges of pan. Serve sliced pieces with Meyer lemon sabayon sauce. Garnish with shaved chocolate.

## Meyer Lemon Sabayon Sauce

5 egg yolks
½ cup plus 2 tablespoons sugar
¼ cup Meyer lemon juice
1 cup heavy cream

Put yolks and ½ cup sugar in a 2-quart mixing bowl that rests snugly on top a slightly larger saucepan. Beat yolks vigorously with a wire whisk or portable electric mixer.

Place 2 inches of water in saucepan and bring to a boil. Do not allow mixing bowl to touch water. Continue beating yolk mixture over boiling water 10 minutes, until yolks are thick and pale yellow.

Remove bowl from saucepan and stir in 2 tablespoons lemon juice. Cool, then refrigerate until thoroughly cold.

Beat cream with remaining sugar until it is almost but not quite stiff. Fold cream into the sauce and stir in remaining lemon juice.

Refrigerate.

*www.theartofrealfood.com*

A couple years ago I decided to experiment by making two angel food cakes, one with organic eggs from the farmers market, the other with ordinary eggs from the grocery store.

Both had good color and baked evenly. But the cake made with organic eggs was two inches taller and had a noticeably sweet-smelling vanilla fragrance. It also had a lighter consistency and a fresher taste.

Food science is not my specialty, but it doesn't take a scientist to convince me to buy organic eggs whenever possible.

Carol Arnold, manager of the Foothill Farmers Market, shared her aunt's angel food cake recipe with us. Who doesn't love angel food cake? It's a healthy dessert, and provides a light and friendly way to top off a meal. For a light nut cake, try the angel food cake with walnuts, page 30.

*From top:*
*Almonds*
*Pecans*
*Pistachios*
*English Walnuts*
*Filberts*

# *january 8*

# Nuts

Spiced Nuts

Chicken, Cranberry and Walnut Wraps

Butterscotch Sauce

Pistachio Meringue Cookies

Angel Food Cake with Walnuts (or Pistachios)

Pistachio Cake

Nuts are packed with nutrients, minerals and vitamins essential for well-being. For example, pistachios are rich in calcium, iron, vitamin A, phosphorus and thiamine. One ounce (¼ cup) of walnuts provides 25 grams of Omega-3, four grams of protein and two grams of fiber. And there is no cholesterol in walnuts. Pecans are an excellent source of vitamin E.

I find nuts, along with a glass of water, make a great afternoon snack, and satisfy my need to grab something to eat before dinner. And when we have guests, there's always a bowl of pistachios in the shell or roasted almonds out for snacking. Both add a touch of salt that nicely complements a glass of wine or juice.

Healthy as they may be, an ounce of nuts has about 190 calories, so limit your daily intake. Remember, all good things in moderation.

# Nuts

## Spiced Nuts

Serves 10 to 12

Preheat oven to 275°F.

2 tablespoons brown sugar
2 teaspoons ground cumin
1 teaspoon baharat
1 teaspoon dried thyme
1 teaspoon salt
1 egg white
1 tablespoon water
1 pound nuts (raw, whole blanched almonds
   work well)

Whisk sugar, spices and salt in a large bowl. Set
aside.

In a medium bowl, whisk egg white and water
until foamy. Add nuts and stir to coat; pour
through a sieve to drain off excess egg. Transfer
nuts to bowl of spices, and stir until evenly
coated.

Line a sheet tray with parchment paper, and
grease lightly with olive oil. Spread mixture
evenly on sheet tray and bake 30 minutes. Reduce
heat to 200°F and bake until dry and golden,
about 30 minutes more. Let cool before serving.

> ℰ₰ Used in Middle Eastern cooking,
> baharat spice is available at Middle Eastern
> markets. The baharat in this recipe is from
> The Spice House, www.thespicehouse.com.
> Or make your own – see recipe page 185.

> ℰ₰ We tried several types of tortillas
> for our wraps. Our favorite was Food for
> Life's Sprouted Grain Tortillas. They're
> all natural, and contain sprouted wheat,
> barley, millet and lentils. We liked the
> seedy texture. Whole wheat tortillas also
> work well for wraps.

## Chicken, Cranberry and Walnut Wraps

Serves 4

4 large tortillas
8 ounces Gina Marie cream cheese
¼ cup dried cranberries
¼ cup walnuts, toasted
2 cups cooked chicken, shredded
¼ cup parsley, chopped
Salt and pepper to taste

For easier rolling, warm tortillas in a dry fry pan
on stove top 15 to 25 seconds.

Spread cream cheese on half of tortilla, and
arrange cranberries, walnuts, chicken and parsley
on other half.

Roll up to and seal edge with a bit more cream
cheese. To serve, cut in half, or slice for
appetizers.

# Butterscotch Sauce

Serves 6 to 8

6 tablespoons butter, melted
⅓ cup white corn syrup
⅔ cup light brown sugar
½ cup heavy cream
1 teaspoon vanilla

Combine butter, corn syrup and brown sugar in a saucepan. Heat until bubbly, and boil 1 minute. Let cool slightly. Add cream and vanilla. Bring mixture to boil, and remove from heat. Cool. Refrigerate, and let cool thoroughly before storing in a tightly sealed jar. To reheat, place sauce in a microwave safe bowl and reheat less than 10 seconds.

# Pistachio Meringue Cookies

Makes 24 small cookies

Preheat oven to 300°F.

3 egg whites, room temperature
⅛ teaspoon salt
1 cup sugar
1 teaspoon vanilla
¾ cup pistachios, finely grated

Beat egg whites and salt until frothy. Slowly add sugar and beat until stiff. Add vanilla and fold in pistachios.
Drop batter by teaspoon onto lightly buttered parchment paper. Bake 25 to 30 minutes.

&✎ A spoonful of butterscotch sauce is great over vanilla bean ice cream or a piece of cake. That didn't happen with this batch of sauce. You see, I made it the morning before a cookbook meeting, and when Chef Laura arrived, I offered her a spoonful to taste. It was buttery and delicious, so we had seconds. Then someone else arrived, and I offered another spoonful. Before we knew it, we were gathered round the bowl sampling until it was all gone. That's one of the advantages of writing a cookbook: you get to sample everything.

## Angel Food Cake with Walnuts (or Pistachios)

Serves 10 to 12

Preheat oven to 350°F.

1 cup cake flour
1½ cups sugar
½ teaspoon salt
1½ cups free-range egg whites (about 12 large eggs), room temperature
1 teaspoon cream of tartar
1 tablespoon lemon juice
1½ teaspoons vanilla extract
1 cup walnuts or pistachios, finely chopped.
1 cup heavy cream, whipped, and 1 tablespoon sugar folded in

Sift flour, then measure, and place in a bowl. Add ½ cup sugar and salt to flour and sift twice more. Set aside.

Beat egg whites in a large, clean bowl. When whites are foamy, add cream of tartar, lemon juice and vanilla extract. When bubbles are uniform, add remaining sugar a few tablespoons at a time. Beat whites until they form stiff peaks (when you lift the beaters a peak will form and hold) and sugar is dissolved.

Fold in flour with a clean rubber spatula, using a down-the-side-and-up-through-the-batter motion. Do not over mix.

Fold in walnuts or pistachios.

When mixture is thoroughly combined, turn into a very clean, grease-free 10-inch tube pan.

Bake 50 minutes. Test for doneness by pressing lightly in center of cake; if it springs back, cake is done. Remove from oven and invert pan until cake is cool.

The cake must be raised an inch or more above the counter during cooling process. An easy way to do this is to invert the cake pan over a wine-type bottle. See photo page 24.

When cool, remove cake by running a serrated knife around edges of pan.

Serve with a dollop of whipped cream. For a nice finish, sprinkle ground walnuts or pistachios or shaved chocolate over top.

# Pistachio Cake

Serves 10 to 12

Preheat oven to 350°F.

3 cups cake flour, sifted before measuring

3 teaspoons baking soda

½ teaspoon salt

¾ cup butter, room temperature

1½ cups sugar

3 eggs, room temperature, separated

1 cup whole milk

1 teaspoon vanilla

1¼ cups unsalted pistachios, finely grated

1 cup heavy cream, whipped

Blend flour, baking soda and salt; sift together. Set aside.

Cream butter and gradually add sugar. Beat until light and airy.

Beat egg yolks and add to butter mixture.

Add flour mixture, milk and vanilla in small amounts into butter mixture and blend until creamy. Set aside.

Whip egg whites until stiff. Fold 1 cup grated pistachios into egg whites. Fold mixture into batter.

Butter two 8x4-inch loaf pans. Divide mixture into each pan.

Bake 30 to 40 minutes. Remove from oven and cool 5 to 10 minutes. Invert onto wire rack to finish cooling.

Serve sliced cake with whipped cream, sprinkled with remaining pistachio nuts.

*Stop eating before you're full. –Michael Pollan*

*january 15*

# Broccoli

Broccoli Cheese Soup

Jerusalem Artichoke, Leek and Potato Soup

Mandarin Mustard Roasted Chicken with Romanesco

Quinoa with Turkey and Broccoli

While all vegetables are good for you, some rise to celebrity status. Among the stars on your plate are the ones called crucifers. The word "crucifer" means "cross-bearer" in Latin, and refers to the cross-like shape of the four-petaled flowers these plants produce. The most widely known crucifer is broccoli, but the family includes cauliflower, cabbage and Brussels sprouts, which form a "head" as they grow. Another branch of the family is called "headless crucifers," and includes dark leafy greens such as kale and collard greens.

Cruciferous vegetables are high in dietary fiber, and delicious sources of vitamins A, B, C, D and E, as well as calcium, iron, magnesium, potassium and zinc. But this alphabet of vitamins and minerals is not what puts these vegetables on the nutritional red carpet. Rather, it's their cancer-fighting compounds. Many studies show that phytochemicals found only in cruciferous vegetables significantly reduce the risk of cancer by stimulating the part of the immune system that fights toxic (carcinogenic) invaders, thus inhibiting the growth or spread of cancerous cells. Researchers are careful to note these vegetables should not be viewed as a fool-proof preventative or as a magical cure. Nonetheless, there are many who would recommend adding cruciferous vegetables to the adage, "An apple a day..."

# Broccoli

## Broccoli Cheese Soup

Serves 8

1 tablespoon olive oil
1 tablespoon butter
1 cup yellow onions, diced
2 cloves garlic, minced
2 heads broccoli, cut into florets
2½ cups vegetable stock
2 cups cream
1 cup cheddar cheese, grated
Salt and pepper to taste

In a large pot, heat oil and butter, add onions
and garlic and cook until fragrant. Add broccoli,
stock and cream. Bring to a boil. Reduce heat to a
simmer and cook until broccoli is tender, about
25 minutes. Remove from heat.
Carefully pour ¼ of the soup into a blender and
pulse to purée. Transfer to a large bowl or
another pot. Continue, working in batches, until
all soup is puréed.
Stir in cheese and season to taste with salt and
pepper.

## Jerusalem Artichoke, Leek and Potato Soup

Serves 8

*Thanks to Courtney McDonald for this recipe.*

½ cup extra virgin olive oil
2 tablespoons unsalted butter
2 leeks, washed and sliced (dark green tops removed)
2 cloves garlic, thinly sliced
1½ pounds potatoes, peeled and quartered
4 pounds Jerusalem artichokes, scrubbed
  or peeled
½ cup heavy cream
Salt and pepper to taste
½ cup sour cream for garnish (optional)

In a medium soup pot, heat olive oil and butter
over medium heat. Add leeks and garlic. Cook,
stirring occasionally, until leeks are soft and
fragrant, about 10 minutes. Do not brown.
Add potatoes and Jerusalem artichokes. Add
enough water to cover vegetables (about 6 to 8
cups). Bring to a boil. Reduce heat and simmer
until potatoes and Jerusalem artichokes are very
soft, about 40 minutes.
Purée soup in batches, and pour into a clean pot.
When done, season to taste with salt and pepper.
Add cream to finish. Re-heat if necessary.
Garnish with a large dollop of sour cream, and
serve with crusty bread. Makes great leftovers.

Jerusalem artichokes are not from Jerusalem, nor are they related to artichokes; the name comes from the Italian word "girasole," which means "sunflower." Also called sunchokes, they produce masses of knobby underground tubers that resemble ginger root. They're available October through March at farmers markets and produce markets.

The tough, strong growing, somewhat coarse-looking plants can reach five or more feet tall, and are covered with masses of small, sunflower-like flowers in the fall. If you grow them yourself, you can dig the tubers as you need them. Any tubers left in the ground will sprout in the spring, giving you another trouble-free crop of these nutty tasting tubers.

# Leftovers are a PLUS!

It makes sense to think about leftovers when you prepare a meal, or even to cook enough so there are leftovers for later. Chances are, there's always something left that would provide a good starting point for another meal. In my family, leftovers are definitely a plus.

So when someone asks what's for dinner, and no one has been shopping for a while, we think about leftovers. The first place to check is the refrigerator. Next, take a peek in the cupboard, or look to see what fruit is on the kitchen counter. And never forget the freezer. With leftover meat, fish, vegetables or fruits, we can always find a way to make a healthy, hearty meal.

The best soups and sandwiches are made with leftovers. And it wouldn't be a stir fry without a few leftover ingredients. One day, for example, I peeked in the fridge and found mushrooms, kale, and a piece of chicken breast. I knew there was homemade chicken broth in the freezer and there are always onions on the counter. Sounds like soup or a stir fry for dinner tonight. For the soup we'll need the chicken broth and orzo pasta, for the stir fry there's surely brown rice in the cupboard.

Not in the mood for soup? How about a green salad with in-season fruit, crumbled blue cheese, pulled chicken breast meat, a quick sweet and sour dressing, all topped with chopped pecans? Eggs in the fridge might end up in an egg salad sandwich or a healthy potato salad with a few freshly diced vegetables.

Don't forget fish. Leftover cooked salmon or crab is a nice beginning for a crostini appetizer, the crostini topped with pieces of fish, a dab of sour cream, a few capers, and some diced onions. Or try salmon and crab tossed with pasta, or pieces of fish on top of a hearty green salad. Or how about crab cakes?

Let your imagination guide you, and you'll be inspired to try new combinations. The end result will satisfy your hunger and leave you pleased knowing leftover foods are not going to waste.

## Mandarin Mustard Roasted Chicken with Romanesco

Serves 6

Preheat oven to 350°F.

1 chicken, 2 to 3 pounds, cut into 6 pieces
2 tablespoons olive oil
Salt and pepper to taste
½ bottle Snow's Citrus Court Mandarin Orange
   Mustard Dressing
4 cups romanesco, cut into florets

Season chicken with 1 tablespoon oil, salt and pepper. Roast 10 to 15 minutes. Glaze with dressing and roast 20 to 25 minutes longer, until juices are clear. Set aside.

Increase temperature to 375°F.

Season romanesco with remaining oil, salt and pepper, and roast in a single layer, 10 to 15 minutes, until edges begin to brown. Serve on a platter with chicken.

# Quinoa with Turkey and Broccoli

Serves 8

Preheat oven to 375°F.

6 tablespoons butter
6 tablespoons flour
3½ cups chicken stock
¾ cup cream
2 teaspoons rosemary, chopped
1 tablespoon thyme
¼ teaspoon nutmeg
Salt and pepper to taste
3½ cups cooked turkey, chopped
2 cups romanesco, cut into small florets
2 cups quinoa, cooked
½ cup bread crumbs
½ cup Parmesan cheese, grated

In a large skillet, melt butter and stir in flour. Continue to cook and stir about 2 minutes, until light beige in color. Gradually add stock and simmer 5 to 7 minutes, stirring frequently. Stir in cream, herbs and spices and season to taste with salt and pepper.

Stir in turkey and romanesco and heat through. Set aside.

Place quinoa in 9x13-inch baking dish and cover with turkey mixture. In a small bowl, combine breadcrumbs and cheese and sprinkle over top. Bake uncovered until bubbly, about 20 minutes. Finish under broiler to brown top.

# *january 22*
# Root Vegetables

Root Vegetable and Flank Steak Stir Fry
Pasties
Roasted Root Vegetables with Mandarin Reduction
Smashed Rutabaga with Love

*P*arsnips, rutabagas and turnips are the most common of the hearty root vegetables that are staple crops during the winter months. When the weather turns cold, root vegetables sound great for dinner. It's as though Nature knows just what our bodies need during the cold months, and provides us with exactly what we need to eat when we need to eat it. Our bodies don't seem to require the full-bodied flavors of root vegetables during the spring and summer months.

Parsnips are similar to carrots but sweeter and more buttery when cooked. Add them to the simmering process when making stews, just like you would carrots. They'll give the stock a rich, deep flavor. Discard them along with the bones when done, leaving just the memory of their taste in the stew.

Rutabaga is a cross between a cabbage and a turnip. Slice them thinly and eat them raw in a salad, add them to soups and stews, or serve them roasted or boiled. Try mashing rutabagas alone or with potatoes; add butter and some cream and serve. Mash them with carrots, or include them in homemade pasties.

The most commonly sold turnips are the white ones. However, it's normal to see tinges of purple, red or green along the tops of the turnips where they were exposed to the sun while growing. Raw turnips have a pungent flavor similar to cabbage or radishes. Tiny turnips are pretty added to a crudités platter; they're milder than their larger cousins. Like other root vegetables, turnips are very adaptable; serve them roasted, fried or steamed.

# Root Vegetables

## Root Vegetable and Flank Steak Stir Fry

Serves 8

2 pounds flank steak, thinly sliced

2 tablespoons olive oil

2 tablespoons balsamic vinegar

2 teaspoons thyme, chopped

2 teaspoons rosemary, chopped

Salt and pepper to taste

1 tablespoon grapeseed oil

4 turnips, peeled and sliced

4 rutabagas, peeled and sliced

1 head broccoli, cut into florets

Steamed brown rice

In a small bowl, combine flank steak, olive oil, vinegar and spices. Cover and marinate 1 hour. Remove steak from marinade. Over medium heat, reduce marinade to ¼ cup. Set aside.

Season steak with salt and pepper to taste.

In a large sauté pan, heat grapeseed oil on high heat. Quickly brown steak on both sides. Remove from pan and place in a bowl. Cover to keep warm.

Sauté vegetables separately the same way, adding to the bowl.

Transfer steak and cooked vegetables back to pan and toss with marinade; check seasoning. Serve over steamed brown rice.

A mixture of ground beef, pork and lamb makes an excellent filling. You can substitute root vegetables for the potatoes.

# Pasties

Serves 8

*Thanks to Jan Christofferson for this recipe.*

Preheat oven to 350°F.

## Crust

4 cups flour
1 cup shortening
1 cup butter
1 tablespoon sugar
2 teaspoons salt
1 tablespoon vinegar
1 egg
½ cup cold water

Mix together flour, shortening, butter, sugar and salt with pastry blender until mixture is the size of small peas. Combine remaining ingredients in another bowl, and then add to flour. Blend until moistened. Form into a ball. Chill dough at least 1 hour before rolling.

## Filling

1½ pounds ground beef
1½ cups celery, diced
¾ cup onions, diced
3 cups potatoes, peeled and diced
Salt and pepper to taste
2 tablespoons butter
1 egg, beaten with 1 teaspoon water

In a large mixing bowl, combine beef, celery, onions and potatoes. Season lightly with salt and pepper. Set aside.
To make pasties: Divide dough into 8 equal pieces. Roll each piece out to approximately ¼-inch thick. Place ½ cup meat mixture on dough, then a dab of butter on meat. Fold dough over. Seal edges.
Brush top with egg wash and cut three slits on top of each pasty to vent.
Place on a sheet tray lined with parchment paper and bake 60 minutes, until golden brown.

# Root Vegetables

## Roasted Root Vegetables with Mandarin Reduction

Serves 6

Preheat oven to 375°F.

1 cup mandarin juice
4 carrots, peeled and cut into 1-inch pieces
2 parsnips, peeled and cut into wedges
2 rutabagas, peeled and cut into wedges
2 golden turnips, peeled and cut into wedges
2 tablespoons olive oil
4 mandarins, segmented
Salt and pepper to taste

In a small saucepan, simmer mandarin juice until reduced to ¼ cup. Set aside.

Season vegetables with olive oil and roast 10 to 20 minutes, until tender. Immediately toss with juice reduction and mandarins. Season to taste with salt and pepper.

# Smashed Rutabaga with Love

Serves 6

Preheat oven to broil.

4 cups rutabaga, peeled and diced
Salt and pepper to taste
¼ cup butter
½ cup sour cream
½ cup Parmesan cheese, grated
¼ cup Gruyère cheese, grated

Place rutabaga in large stock pot and cover with water. Season lightly with salt and bring to a boil. Reduce heat and simmer 15 to 25 minutes, until fork tender. Drain and return to pot. Smash with a potato masher and stir in remaining ingredients. Add more salt and pepper if desired. Transfer to baking dish, and broil until golden brown.

Love is any ingredient added to a recipe that makes you feel good. It can be extra butter, cream, cheese, even chocolate. It's a little something that gives the dish an extra punch, an unexpected flavor, or a bit of richness. And since we don't count calories when adding extra love, we suggest you save this for extra special occasions.

*january 29*

# Cauliflower

Cauliflower Soup

Steamed Cauliflower with Cheese Sauce

Roasted Cauliflower with Lemon and Pine Nuts

Spicy Anise and Ginger Reduction

The colors and tastes of winter vegetables are a feast for the eye as well as the palate. Cauliflower is a star performer. Imagine a platter of crudités with snowy white cauliflower florets, light green Romanesco flowers, red and green watermelon radishes, orange carrot slices and dark green celery stalks. Garnish with celery leaves. What could be more beautiful?

Add two or three small bowls of home-made dip, and you have a lovely and healthy way to begin your meal.

# Cauliflower

## Cauliflower Soup

Serves 8

1 tablespoon butter
½ onion, diced
3 cups cauliflower, cut into florets
2 cups chicken or vegetable stock
2 cups half and half
Salt and pepper to taste
½ cup Gruyère cheese, grated (optional)
2 tablespoons parsley, chopped

In a large pot, heat butter and add onions. Cook until fragrant, and add cauliflower. Stir to combine, and add stock and half and half. Season lightly with salt and pepper and bring to a boil. Reduce heat to simmer, and cook until cauliflower is tender, about 25 to 35 minutes. Transfer to blender and process until smooth. Check seasoning. Garnish with Gruyère cheese and parsley.

## Steamed Cauliflower with Cheese Sauce

Serves 4

1 head cauliflower, cut into florets
1½ cups cream
¼ cup Gruyère cheese, grated
Salt and pepper to taste

Steam cauliflower until tender. Set aside.
To make cheese sauce: In a small saucepan, simmer cream until reduced by half. Remove from heat and stir in cheese to melt. Season to taste with salt and pepper.
Serve cauliflower with cheese sauce.

> Use a hand blender for hot soups and sauces. It's easier, safer and less messy. However, if you want a really smooth finished product, use a food processor or blender.

# Roasted Cauliflower with Lemon and Pine Nuts

Serves 4

Preheat oven to 375°F.

1 head cauliflower, cut into florets
1 tablespoon olive oil
Salt and pepper to taste
¼ cup Parmesan cheese, grated
¼ cup pine nuts
1 lemon, zested

Toss cauliflower with oil, salt and pepper. Roast on a sheet tray 15 to 20 minutes, until tender and beginning to brown.
Mix Parmesan, nuts and zest together. Add cauliflower, toss, adjust seasoning and serve.

# Spicy Anise and Ginger Reduction

Makes 6 cups

4 cups sugar
4 cups distilled or filtered water
8 cinnamon sticks
28 whole cloves
1 cup fresh ginger, peeled, thinly sliced
20 green cardamom seeds
16 whole star anise

In 2-quart sauce pan, dissolve sugar in water and bring to a boil. Add spices. Simmer 10 minutes. Remove from heat, cover pan, and let steep 30 minutes.
Using a sieve, strain spices and discard.
Return sauce to pan, bring to a boil, and simmer 20 minutes. When cool, place in a covered jar and store in the refrigerator.

Use this Spicy Anise and Ginger Reduction to flavor sparkling wine, juices, and sauces. A tablespoon adds a punch to rhubarb and blackberry sauce, a glass of Prosecco, or unsweetened apple juice. Try it. I guarantee you'll like it.

*February 5*

# Fennel

Fennel and Apple Soup

Fennel, Beet and Orange Salad

Roasted Chicken with Fennel and Snap Peas

Pink Rice with Sand Dabs

Lasagna with Dungeness Crab, Fennel and Mushrooms

Fennel, or sweet anise, has a bulbous base and long stalks topped with airy fern-like fronds. It has a light licorice taste and aroma. The Italians prefer raw fennel dipped in olive oil and sprinkled with sea salt.

Roast it with a bit of olive oil; serve it sautéed with slices of duck or pork. And if added to soup just before serving, it delivers not only a slight crunch but a subtle flavor. Use the feathery tops as garnish.

# Fennel

## Fennel and Apple Soup

Serves 6

1 tablespoon butter
3 apples, cored and sliced
1 medium fennel bulb, diced
1 onion, sliced
4 stalks celery with leaves, chopped
Salt and pepper to taste
3 cups stock
½ cup dry white wine
1 lemon, juiced
½ cup bacon, diced and cooked
6 fennel fronds for garnish

Heat butter in a large saucepan, and add apple, fennel, onions and celery. Cook until fragrant and season lightly with salt and pepper. Add stock and wine. Simmer 20 minutes, until all are tender.
Purée soup in a blender until smooth and strain through a mesh strainer; return to pot. Whisk in lemon juice and check seasoning.
Return to simmer before serving. Garnish with bacon and fennel fronds.

## Fennel, Beet and Orange Salad

Serves 4

Preheat oven to 400°F.

2 bunches beets
2 tablespoons olive oil
Salt and pepper to taste
2 tablespoons orange juice
1 large fennel bulb, thinly sliced
3 oranges, segmented
Fennel fronds for garnish

Coat beets lightly with 1 tablespoon oil, salt and pepper, and place in roasting pan. Cover with foil and roast 25 to 35 minutes, until fork tender. Cool slightly; peel and discard skins. Cut into ¼-inch slices and place directly on serving plates. In a small bowl, whisk together orange juice, remaining oil, salt and pepper to taste. Set aside. Combine fennel and oranges, toss with dressing, and arrange on top of sliced beets. Garnish with fennel fronds if desired.

*Plant a vegetable garden if you have the space, a window box if you don't.*
  *–Michael Pollan*

# Roasted Chicken with Fennel and Snap Peas

Serves 6

Preheat oven to 350°F.

1 whole chicken, 2 to 3 pounds
1 tablespoon olive oil
Salt and pepper to taste
1 lemon, halved
3 sprigs thyme
1 sprig rosemary
2 tablespoons grapeseed oil
2 cloves garlic, minced
2 large fennel bulbs, thinly sliced
1 pound snap peas, cleaned
Fennel fronds for garnish (optional)

Season chicken with olive oil, salt and pepper. Place lemon and herbs inside cavity. Roast 45 to 60 minutes, until legs are loose and juices are clear.
In a large sauté pan, heat grapeseed oil and cook garlic until fragrant. Add fennel and continue to cook until slightly caramelized. Add peas and toss to cook until tender. Season to taste with salt and pepper.
Arrange vegetables on a large platter. Place chicken on top. Garnish with fennel fronds if desired.

# Pink Rice with Sand Dabs

Serves 4

2 cups pink rice
3½ cups water
Salt and pepper to taste
1 tablespoon butter
1 clove garlic, minced
¼ cup onions, diced
1 large fennel bulb, diced
1 lemon, juiced
2 tablespoons grapeseed oil
1 to 1½ pounds sand dabs, cleaned, skin on

Heat rice and water in a medium saucepan, and season lightly with salt and pepper.
Bring to a boil, reduce heat, cover and simmer 20 to 25 minutes, until tender.
In a large sauté pan, heat butter, and cook garlic and onions until fragrant. Add fennel and continue to cook until tender.
In a large bowl, mix together cooked rice and fennel mixture with lemon juice and season to taste with salt and pepper. Set aside.
Heat oil in a large sauté pan. Dry fish on a paper towel, season with salt and pepper, and then sear, skin-side-down until crisp, about 2 minutes. Flip fish, turn off heat and finish cooking.
Serve fish on bed of rice.

# Fennel

## Lasagna with Dungeness Crab, Fennel and Mushrooms

Serves 10 to 12

*This recipe inspired by Robert Schneider's recipe in "The Open Hand Cookbook."*

Preheat oven to 325°F.

4 cups heavy cream

¼ cup olive oil

2 medium fennel bulbs, tops removed, sliced ¼-inch thick (dice fronds and add to slices)

⅔ pound young Swiss chard, sliced ½-inch thick

¼ cup water

5 shallots, chopped medium fine

1½ pounds crimini mushrooms, cut into broad, thin slices

½ cup dry sherry

3 pounds ripe tomatoes, coarsely chopped, or two 28-ounce cans of organic diced tomatoes

3 sprigs fresh tarragon, stems removed, leaves coarsely chopped

Salt and pepper to taste

4 sheets fresh pasta, 9x12 inches each

2 cups Parmesan cheese, grated

1½ pounds Dungeness crab meat, freshly cooked

In a large saucepan, simmer cream until reduced by half. Set aside.

In a large skillet, heat 2 tablespoons olive oil. Add fennel and sauté 2 to 3 minutes. Add chard and water. Cover and steam until fennel and chard are wilted, about 2 to 3 minutes. Discard water. Remove fennel and chard. Set aside.

In the same skillet, add remaining oil and sauté shallots 2 to 3 minutes, until soft. Add mushrooms and continue cooking until mushrooms release their liquid, about 2 to 3 minutes more. Add sherry and cook an additional 2 to 3 minutes. Remove mushrooms and set aside.

Add more olive oil to skillet if necessary. Increase heat to high, and add tomatoes and tarragon. Cook until the tomatoes are very soft and most liquid has evaporated. Add the reduced cream and season with salt and pepper. Cook 2 to 3 minutes, and remove from heat. When done, sauce should be thick enough to stick to the back of a spoon, and if you rub your finger across it, it leaves a line.

Pour ¼ cup of sauce in 10x15-inch lasagna pan. Cover with first sheet of pasta dough. Top with drained chard and fennel, then spoon ½ cup sauce over vegetables and sprinkle with Parmesan cheese. Cover with second sheet of pasta, and top with shallot and mushroom mixture. Spoon ½ cup sauce over mushrooms and shallots, and sprinkle with Parmesan cheese. Cover with another sheet of pasta. Layer fresh crabmeat with a generous amount of sauce, and finally, add the last sheet of pasta, the rest of the sauce and more Parmesan cheese.

Cover lasagna with a sheet of parchment paper, then foil. Crimp edges to seal securely.

Bake 35 to 45 minutes, until hot throughout.

# Basic Pasta Recipe

Makes 4 9x12-inch pieces

*Thanks to Tyler Florence for this basic pasta recipe.*

2 cups all purpose flour, plus more for dusting
1 teaspoon salt
3 eggs
2 tablespoons olive oil

Combine flour and salt on a flat work surface; shape into a mound and make a well in the center. Add eggs and olive oil to well, and lightly beat with a fork. Gradually draw flour from inside well wall in a circular motion. Use your hand for mixing, being careful to protect the outer wall. Continue to incorporate flour until it forms a ball. Sprinkle a dusting of flour on work surface, knead and fold dough until elastic and smooth, about 10 minutes. Wrap dough in plastic wrap; let rest about 30 minutes to allow gluten to relax. To roll out, cut dough into 4 pieces and process through pasta machine, starting with the largest setting and working your way down, gradually making a thinner sheet with each pass. We used a hand-crank machine, and finished on setting 3. Place rolled sheets of pasta on a sheet tray lined with flour or cornmeal. Keep covered until ready to use.

Pam Wilson delivered this crab lasagna to me as I recovered from surgery; the meal was so delicious I asked her to come over so we could make it together and add the recipe to this cookbook. Everyone will want the recipe.

*February 12*

# Endive

Warm Endive Salad with Pine Nuts
Endive and Fennel Salad with Mandarin and Meyer Lemon Vinaigrette
Seared Pork Chops with Endive
Endive Jambon
Braised Endives

We think of dirt as inert. Technically, that's correct. Dirt is actually dead, but soil is teeming with life. A teaspoon of healthy soil can contain billions of microbes. A handful of soil can contain earthworms, centipedes, beetles and countless other creatures.

All these organisms contribute to a complex ecosystem that creates, renews and fortifies the soil that feeds plants. In turn, plants and the animals that feed on them provide organic matter to feed the soil. In an undisturbed setting, such as a forest, this symbiotic cycle takes care of itself. When we remove plants, as we do with agriculture, we interrupt that cycle. On the most basic of levels, we're removing nutrients before they can be restored.

Small scale and organic farmers who typically sell through farmers markets tend to practice farming in a way that replenishes the soil, keeping our food, our soil and our planet healthy.

# Endive

## Warm Endive Salad with Pine Nuts

Serves 4

1 tablespoon Dijon mustard
1 tablespoon red wine vinegar
2 teaspoons lemon juice
3 tablespoons olive oil
Salt and pepper to taste
⅓ cup pine nuts
6 endives, cut crosswise into rings
1 tablespoon parsley, chopped

To make dressing: In a medium bowl, combine mustard, vinegar, and lemon juice. Slowly whisk in oil until dressing is emulsified and season lightly with salt and pepper. Set aside.
Heat a large sauté pan over medium heat and toast pine nuts until golden brown, stirring constantly to prevent burning. Add endive and toss to warm. Add dressing and continue to toss over heat until leaves are wilted. Add more salt and pepper if desired. To serve, garnish with parsley.

*Avoid foods containing ingredients that no ordinary human would keep in the pantry.*
*—Michael Pollan*

## Endive and Fennel Salad with Mandarin and Meyer Lemon Vinaigrette

Serves 4

¼ cup pecans
2 medium fennel bulbs, thinly sliced
4 endives, cut into ½-inch pieces
½ pomegranate, seeded
2 mandarins, segmented
Salt and pepper to taste

### Mandarin and Meyer Lemon Vinaigrette

¼ cup mandarin juice
2 tablespoons Meyer lemon juice
3 tablespoons olive oil

In a large sauté pan, toast pecans until just browned. Add fennel and endive and toss until heated.
In a bowl, whisk vinaigrette ingredients together, add to pan and cook 1 to 2 minutes. Toss with pomegranate seeds and mandarins; season to taste with salt and pepper.

# Seared Pork Chops with Endive

Serves 4

Preheat oven to 200°F.

2 tablespoons grapeseed oil
4 pork chops
Salt and pepper to taste
½ bottle Snow's Citrus Court Mandarin Orange
  Mustard Dressing
1 tablespoon butter
1 tablespoon olive oil
8 endives, cut into quarters, lengthwise

In a large sauté pan, heat grapeseed oil. Season pork chops with salt and pepper and sear on both sides. Just before chops are completely seared, coat with dressing and continue cooking 2 to 3 minutes. Remove from pan. Keep warm in oven.

Heat butter and olive oil in same pan, and sauté endive until it begins to caramelize. Add salt and pepper.

To serve, place pork chops on bed of endive on a large platter.

# Endive

## Endive Jambon

Serves 4 to 6

Preheat oven to 375°F.

12 endives
12 ham slices
¼ cup flour
¼ cup butter
1 quart whole milk
½ pound Gruyère cheese, grated
1 teaspoon nutmeg
Salt and pepper

Place endives vertically in a deep saucepan with 1 inch of water in the bottom. Cover pan and bring to a gentle boil, cooking 30 to 35 minutes, until endives are very tender. Remove from pan and drain.

Allow endives to cool slightly. Gently squeeze to remove any moisture, then wrap each endive in a slice of ham and place in a single layer in a 9x13-inch baking dish. Set aside.

In a saucepan melt butter then whisk in flour to create a smooth roux. Stir constantly while cooking 3 to 4 minutes over low heat. Do not overcook.

Continue stirring and slowly add milk. Increase heat slightly and cook until smooth and thick. Remove from heat.

Season with nutmeg and about ¾ of grated Gruyère cheese, whisking it into warm sauce until melted. Season to taste with salt and pepper.

Pour sauce evenly over wrapped endives. Sprinkle remaining cheese on top.

Bake 30 to 40 minutes, until sauce bubbles. Increase heat, and broil until top golden brown. Serve immediately. Wonderful with mashed potatoes.

> Endive Jambon is a classic Flemish winter dish. It's easy to prepare and delicious.

# Don't overdo it!

Ideal internal temperatures (Fahrenheit)
for cooking reliably-sourced grassfed and pastured meats

| Meat | Suggested Temperatures for Grassfed Meat | USDA Recommended Temperatures |
|---|---|---|
| Beef & Bison | 120–140° | 145–170° |
| Ground Meat | 160° | 160° |
| Veal | 125–155° | 145–170° |
| Lamb & Goat | 120–145° | 145–170° |
| Pork | 145–160° | 160–170° |
| Chicken (unstuffed) | 165° | 165° |
| Turkey (unstuffed) | 165° | 165° |

www.grassfedcooking.com

# Braised Endives

Serves 4

1 pound endives, halved lengthwise
⅓ cup chicken stock
2 tablespoons milk
1 tablespoon mandarin juice
1 tablespoon butter

*Shop the peripheries of the supermarket.
Stay out of the middle.* —Michael Pollan

Place endives in a saucepan and add chicken stock and milk. Cover and cook 10 minutes, over medium heat.
Add mandarin juice and butter. Cover, reduce heat and simmer 20 minutes, until tender.
Turn this dish into a full meal by topping with diced, cooked bacon and your favorite cheese. We suggest Pt. Reyes blue cheese. Serve with artisan bread.

## February 19

# Oranges

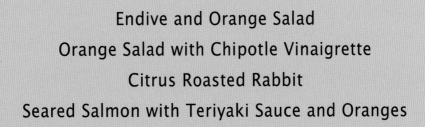

Endive and Orange Salad

Orange Salad with Chipotle Vinaigrette

Citrus Roasted Rabbit

Seared Salmon with Teriyaki Sauce and Oranges

*R*eal, lasting beauty starts at the end of your fork. Vitamin C (strawberries, citrus, and broccoli) aids in the production of collagen, which is the support structure for our skin. Vitamin A (squash, sweet potatoes and spinach) helps keep skin smooth. Zinc and iron (beef, poultry and beans) promote natural sloughing, which keeps skin vibrant. Vitamin E (nuts, dark leafy vegetables and tomatoes) provides natural sun protection.

This list is by no means exhaustive, but helps make two important points. First, nature seasonally provides everything you need for beautiful skin, strong nails and shiny hair. Second, the nutrients that keep us looking young and healthy actually make us healthy. When you eat well, you look well because you are well.

# Oranges

## Endive & Orange Salad

Serves 4

Preheat oven to 300°F.

¼ cup walnuts, chopped
1 tablespoon unseasoned rice vinegar
¼ teaspoon salt
1 teaspoon Dijon mustard
3 tablespoons olive oil
1 tablespoon parsley, finely chopped
Salt and pepper to taste
2 small oranges, segmented
3 each red and white endives
¼ cup Parmesan cheese, grated

Roast walnuts on a sheet tray 12 to 15 minutes, until golden brown. Set aside.
Place vinegar, salt and mustard in a bowl and whisk together. Slowly add oil, whisking until fully combined. Add parsley and season to taste with salt and pepper. Gently fold in oranges. Set aside.
Trim ¼ inch from bottom of endives and remove whole leaves. Repeat as necessary to remove interior leaves. Discard center core section.
Place leaves, cheese and walnuts in salad bowl. Dress with vinegar mixture and toss.

## Orange Salad with Chipotle Vinaigrette

Serves 4

4 oranges, segmented
4 mandarins, segmented

**Chipotle Vinaigrette**
1 tablespoon honey
½ teaspoon chipotle pepper
2 tablespoons olive oil
1 tablespoon apple cider vinegar
Salt and pepper to taste

Combine salad ingredients. Set aside.
In a small bowl, whisk together honey, chipotle, oil and vinegar. Season to taste with salt and pepper. Toss with oranges and serve immediately.

## Citrus Roasted Rabbit

Serves 8

Preheat oven to 400°F.

1 cup orange juice
2 lemons, juiced
2 teaspoons fennel pollen
Pinch saffron
1 teaspoon cayenne
¼ cup honey
2 rabbits, cut into 6 pieces each
Salt and pepper to taste

Combine juices, spices and honey and pour over rabbit. Marinate 1 hour.
Place in a roasting pan and season to taste with salt and pepper.
Roast 20 to 25 minutes, basting halfway through.

# Seared Salmon with Teriyaki Sauce and Oranges

Serves 6

¼ cup soy sauce
¼ cup mirin
1 tablespoon sugar
3 oranges, segmented, reserve juice
Salt and pepper to taste
Cornstarch slurry if needed
2 tablespoons grapeseed oil
1½ pounds salmon filet, cut into 6 equal portions
4 ounces pea shoots

In a small saucepan, combine soy sauce, mirin and sugar, and bring to a boil. Reduce heat and simmer 5 minutes. Add 1 tablespoon orange juice and season to taste with salt and pepper. If desired, thicken with cornstarch slurry.* Set aside.

In a large sauté pan, heat oil. Season fish with salt and pepper, and sear, presentation-side down. When cooked about ⅓ through, flip filets, cook less than 1 minute, and remove from heat. To serve, spoon about ¼ of the sauce on a platter, arrange salmon on top, and garnish with pea shoots and orange segments. Serve remaining sauce in a gravy boat.

*Make a cornstarch slurry by whisking one tablespoon corn starch into ½ cup water. Add a little at a time to the saucepan; bring liquid to a boil to check thickness. Repeat if necessary until mixture is desired thickness.*

# February 26

# Cabbage

Spicy Nutty Jicama Slaw with Lime Ancho Dressing
Sausage Wrapped in Cabbage Leaves
Pork Chops with Sauerkraut and Mashed Potatoes
Roast Beef with Fennel Pollen and Baby Bok Choy

*D*id the Germans invent sauerkraut, or is it a favorite because brined cabbage was a winter staple on mid-western farms? Certainly, sauerkraut with mashed potatoes was comfort food at the dinner table on the Minnesota farm where I grew up. The farm was homesteaded by my German great-grandparents. My parents raised pork, and it was the meat of choice to eat with sauerkraut. For me, it's still perfect on a chilly winter evening.

Our favorite sauerkraut is made by Bubbies. Packed in 25-ounce jars, it's just the right amount for four servings. Best of all, Bubbies sauerkraut is fermented the old-fashioned way: no sugar, no vinegar, and no preservatives. Visit bubbies.com to learn more.

# Cabbage

## Spicy Nutty Jicama Slaw with Lime Ancho Dressing

Serves 6 to 8

1 two-pound jicama, peeled and julienne
½ head Napa cabbage, finely shredded
2 carrots, grated
⅓ cup cilantro leaves, chopped
⅓ cup salted peanuts or cashews,
  coarsely chopped

### Lime Ancho Dressing

2 tablespoons rice vinegar
⅓ cup fresh lime juice
1 tablespoon ancho chili powder (2 tablespoons
  for extra spicy)
2 tablespoons honey or agave syrup
½ cup vegetable oil
Salt and pepper to taste

Combine salad ingredients. Whisk dressing ingredients together and dress salad just before serving.

# Sausage Wrapped in Cabbage Leaves

Serves 4

Preheat oven to 350°F.

4 large cabbage leaves
1 tablespoon grapeseed oil
½ cup onions, small diced
½ cup bell pepper, small diced
1 pound ground pork sausage
Salt and pepper to taste
1 cup tomato sauce
1 teaspoon chili flakes
1 teaspoon fennel pollen

In a large pot of boiling, salted water, blanch cabbage leaves for 30 seconds. Immediately transfer to an ice bath to cool. Lay flat on a paper towel to dry.

In a large sauté pan, heat oil, and cook onions and bell peppers until fragrant. Add sausage and cook until done. Season to taste with salt and pepper. Set aside.

In a saucepan, heat tomato sauce, season with chili flakes and fennel pollen. Simmer to combine flavors, about 10 minutes.

To assemble, place ¼ of sausage mixture at the top center of each cabbage leaf. Roll in and up (like an eggroll) to seal.

Place tomato sauce mixture in baking dish, and place cabbage rolls on top. Bake 10 to 15 minutes before serving.

*Buy smaller plates and glasses. We don't have to supersize portions at home, and shouldn't. One researcher found that simply switching from a 12-inch to a 10-inch dinner plate caused people to reduce their consumption by 22%.*
*–Michael Pollan*

# Cabbage

## Pork Chops with Sauerkraut and Mashed Potatoes

Serves 4

2½ pounds German Butterball or Yukon Gold
  potatoes, quartered

2 tablespoons butter

Salt and pepper to taste

2 to 3 tablespoons half and half, warmed

1 tablespoon grapeseed oil

4 half-pound pork chops, bone in, room
  temperature

1 medium onion, halved and sliced

1 jar (25 ounces) Bubbies sauerkraut

Cook potatoes until easily pierced by a fork,
about 35 to 40 minutes. Drain water and slightly
dry potatoes uncovered over low heat. Add
butter, salt and pepper to potatoes; mash with a
hand mixer or potato masher. Blend in half and
half. Cover pan and keep potatoes hot until pork
chops are done.

Heat stainless steel skillet until hot; add
grapeseed oil. Lightly salt chops and brown 1½ to
2 minutes on each side. Set aside on a plate.
Place onion slices in skillet and sauté until lightly
browned. Sprinkle ½ teaspoon salt over onions.
Place half the sauerkraut on top of onions, and
return chops to skillet.

Add remaining sauerkraut and juices on top of
pork chops. Cover and simmer 30 minutes. Every
10 minutes take juices from bottom of skillet and
spoon over sauerkraut.

To serve, place a large spoonful of mashed
potatoes on a plate. Put a pork chop next to
potatoes and spoon the sauerkraut over potatoes
and pork chop.

# Roast Beef with Fennel Pollen and Baby Bok Choy

Serves 8

Preheat oven to 400°F.

1 sirloin tip roast, 3 to 4 pounds
1 tablespoon olive oil
3 cloves garlic, chopped
2 teaspoons fennel pollen
1 tablespoon thyme
Salt and pepper to taste
1 onion, large diced
2 carrots, quartered
1 tablespoon grapeseed oil
1 clove garlic
6 heads baby bok choy, halved
Salt and pepper to taste

Season roast with olive oil, garlic, fennel pollen, thyme, salt and pepper. Set aside.
Put onions and carrots on sheet tray.
Place roast on top, and bake 10 minutes. Reduce heat to 325°F and continue to cook until medium rare, about 40 minutes, depending on the size. Let rest before slicing. Discard onions and carrots; they were used to add flavor and fragrance to the roast.
In a large sauté pan, heat grapeseed oil and add garlic. Add bok choy; sauté until tender and begins to caramelize. Season to taste with salt and pepper.
To serve, slice beef and arrange on a large platter with bok choy.

*March 5*

# Beets

Roasted Beet Salad with Cucumbers

Pickled Beets

Roasted Beets with Bacon Vinaigrette

Chocolate Beet Cake

*Don't get your fuel from the same place your car does.* —Michael Pollan

## Roasted Beet Salad with Cucumbers

Serves 4

Preheat oven to 400°F.

1 pound beets
1 tablespoon olive oil
Salt and pepper to taste
2 cups Persian cucumbers, sliced ¼-inch thick
2 ounces goat cheese
2 tablespoons red wine vinegar
1 tablespoon olive oil
Dill sprigs for garnish

Place beets in a roasting pan, coat with oil and season lightly with salt and pepper. Cover with foil and roast 25 to 35 minutes, until fork tender. Let cool slightly and peel off skins, trim ends and slice into wedges. Toss with remaining ingredients and serve. Garnish with dill.

# Beets

## Pickled Beets

Serves 8 to 10

3 pounds beets
Salt and pepper to taste
1 red onion, julienne
2 cups Champagne vinegar
¾ cup sugar
1 tablespoon salt
1 tablespoon pickling spice
Dill sprigs for garnish

Place beets in a large pot, cover with water and season with salt. Bring to a boil, then reduce heat and simmer until beets are fork tender. Drain water and let cool slightly. Peel off skins, trim ends and slice into wedges. Combine beet wedges with onions. Set aside.

Heat vinegar, sugar, salt and pickling spice in a small saucepan. When sugar is dissolved, strain over sliced beets and onions, season to taste with salt and pepper, and garnish with dill.

## Roasted Beets with Bacon Vinaigrette

Serves 6

Preheat oven to 400°F.

2 bunches beets, stems trimmed
1 tablespoon olive oil
Salt and pepper to taste
6 pieces bacon, diced
3 cups mixed greens
2 oranges, segmented
2 ounces Pt. Reyes blue cheese, crumbled

### Bacon Vinaigrette
2 tablespoons reserved bacon fat
1 tablespoon red wine vinegar
1 tablespoon olive oil
1 teaspoon Dijon mustard

Place beets in a roasting pan, coat with oil and season lightly with salt and pepper. Cover with foil and roast 25 to 35 minutes, until fork tender. Let cool slightly and peel off skins, trim ends and slice into wedges. Set aside.
In a medium sauté pan, cook bacon until just crisp. Remove from pan; drain and reserve fat. Combine all vinaigrette ingredients and season to taste with salt and pepper.
In a medium bowl, toss greens with half of vinaigrette and place on platter.
Toss beets and bacon together with remaining vinaigrette, and serve on top of greens. Garnish with oranges and cheese.

# Chocolate Beet Cake

Serves 8 to 10

Preheat oven to 350°F.

1¾ cups all purpose flour

1½ teaspoons baking soda

⅓ teaspoon salt

1 can (15 ounces) quartered or diced beets, drained, liquid reserved

1 cup sugar

1 cup vegetable oil

½ cup beet juice (drained from can of beets)

3 large eggs

1 teaspoon vanilla extract

4 ounces Sweet Earth unsweetened chocolate, melted

1 cup Sweet Earth semi-sweet chocolate chips

Place flour, baking soda and salt in a medium bowl. Blend and set aside.

Purée drained beets in a food processor. Place in a large bowl and add sugar, vegetable oil, and beet juice. Mix with a hand mixer until blended. Add eggs and vanilla, and continue beating until mixed.

Add flour mixture to the beet mixture. Blend together. Add melted chocolate and mix until well blended.

Pour into buttered 9x13-inch baking pan.

Sprinkle chocolate chips evenly over the top of the batter.

Bake 40 to 45 minutes, until toothpick inserted in middle of baking pan comes out clean. Cool to room temperature before slicing.

We use Sweet Earth Chocolates (sweetearthchocolates.com), whose 65% chocolate scored highest in the San Francisco Chronicle's blind chocolate tasting. Based in San Luis Obispo, this chocolatier has more than flavor to recommend it. All their chocolate is certified organic and Fair Trade, which means the cocoa beans they use are produced in a way that does no harm to the planet or the farmer. A portion of their profits supports Project Hope and Fairness, a non-profit organization that promotes the sustainability of African cocoa farmers and their communities.

*Avoid foods you see advertised on television.*
*—Michael Pollan*

*From the top:*
*Mountain Rose*
*Yukon Gold*
*Romance*
*German Butterball*
*Rose Finn*
*Yellow Finn*
*Russet*

# Potatoes

Potato and Green Bean Salad

Pickled Herring with Mashed Potatoes and Onions

Roasted Romanesco and German Butterball Potato Mash

Chicken Fried Steak with Mashed Potatoes

Potatoes au Gratin

Stuffed Baked Potatoes with Romanesco

## Potato and Green Bean Salad

Serves 6

¾ pound green beans, cut in 3-inch pieces
1 pound Yukon Gold potatoes, peeled,
   diced in 1-inch cubes
2 cloves garlic, minced
1 teaspoon chili flakes
3 tablespoons olive oil
1 tablespoon red wine vinegar
1 teaspoon lemon zest
1 tablespoon lemon juice
1 bunch radishes, sliced
2 teaspoons parsley, chopped
Salt and pepper to taste

Blanch green beans in a pot of boiling, salted water for 30 seconds, and then transfer to a bowl of ice water to chill. Set aside.
In a large pot of water, gently boil potatoes until fork tender. Drain completely.

Whisk together garlic, chili flakes, oil, vinegar, zest and juice, and dress potatoes while still hot. Toss potatoes with green beans, radishes and parsley. Season to taste with salt and pepper. Best served at room temperature.

# Potatoes

## Pickled Herring with Mashed Potatoes and Onions

Serves 6

2½ pounds German Butterball or Yukon Gold
  potatoes, quartered
2 tablespoons butter
Salt and pepper to taste
2 to 3 tablespoons half and half, warmed
2 teaspoons olive oil
2 cups onions, julienne
6 to 8 ounces pickled herring fillets in
  wine, drained

Place potatoes in a small amount of water, and cook until easily pierced with a fork, 35 to 40 minutes. Drain water and slightly dry potatoes uncovered over low heat. Add butter, salt and pepper; mash with hand mixer or potato masher. Blend in half and half. Cover pan and keep potatoes hot.

Heat oil in frying pan; add onions and sauté slowly until slightly caramelized.

To serve: Place a large spoonful of mashed potatoes on a plate. Top with spoonful of caramelized onions, and place 4 or 5 herring filets on the edge.

## Roasted Romanesco and German Butterball Potato Mash

Serves 6

Preheat oven to 400°F.

3 cups romanesco, cut into florets
1 tablespoon olive oil
Salt and pepper to taste
2 pounds German Butterball potatoes, halved
¼ cup butter

In a large bowl, toss romanesco with olive oil and season lightly with salt and pepper. Roast on a baking sheet until deeply caramelized, about 20 to 30 minutes.

Meanwhile, cook potatoes in salted water until fork tender. Drain and let dry.

Pass potatoes through a mill with butter. Add romanesco, stir to combine, and season to taste with salt and pepper.

---

❧ Use leftover mashed potatoes to thicken soup. Add in ½ cup increments. You can also grate a raw potato, add it to the soup, and it will thicken the soup as it cooks.

---

❧ Pickled herring is an acquired taste. Growing up, I had several Scandinavian relatives who enjoyed eating preserved fish, so I learned early to appreciate the distinctive flavors of herring and sardines.

Did you know salmon and herring contain some of the highest levels of Omega-3 fatty acids? Research shows eating one fish meal per week can reduce your risk of heart disease, and nutritional experts recommend consuming fish two or three times a week.

For keeping foods hot without burning, use a stove-top heat diffuser. It's great for mashed potatoes and other vegetables that need to stay hot, but not continue cooking, until meal time.

## Chicken Fried Steak with Mashed Potatoes and Gravy

Serves 6

Preheat oven to 300°F.

2½ pounds German Butterball or Yukon Gold
   potatoes, quartered
¼ cup butter
Salt and pepper to taste
2 to 3 tablespoons half and half, warmed
2 pounds beef bottom round, sliced ½-inch thick
1 cup flour, seasoned with salt and pepper
3 eggs, beaten
3 tablespoons grapeseed oil
2 cups chicken stock
½ cup half and half
1 teaspoon thyme, chopped

Place potatoes in a small amount of water, and cook until easily pierced with a fork, 35 to 40 minutes. Drain water and slightly dry potatoes uncovered over low heat. Add 2 tablespoons butter, and salt and pepper; mash with a hand mixer or potato masher. Blend in half and half.

Cover pan and keep potatoes hot.

Dredge each slice of beef in flour; shake off excess, and pound to tenderize between two pieces of plastic wrap. Dredge again in flour, then egg, then flour, and place in a single layer on a sheet tray. Refrigerate 10 minutes.

Heat oil in a large sauté pan and fry meat on both sides, until golden brown, about 3 to 4 minutes per side. Place wire cooling rack on top of sheet tray, and cool meat on rack. Repeat until all meat is fried.

To make gravy, wipe pan clean, and add remaining butter. Stir in 3 tablespoons of dredging flour, and cook over low heat until combined, 2 to 3 minutes. Add stock, bring to a boil while whisking until smooth. Reduce heat to simmer, add half and half and thyme; season to taste with salt and pepper. Simmer 2 to 3 minutes longer.

Serve meat with mashed potatoes and gravy.

*Go food shopping every week. –Michael Pollan*

# Potatoes

The difference between scalloped and au gratin potatoes is in the cheese. Traditional scalloped potatoes are made with a cream sauce; au gratin potatoes are made with the same sauce plus cheese.

## Potatoes au Gratin

Serves 8

Preheat oven to 350°F.

¼ cup butter
2 cups onions, sliced
10 Yukon Gold potatoes, peeled and
   sliced ¼-inch thick
2 cups chicken stock
2 cups cream
Salt and pepper to taste
1 cup Parmesan cheese, grated
1½ cups breadcrumbs
½ cup asiago cheese, grated

Heat 2 tablespoons butter in a large sauté pan and cook onions over medium heat. Reduce heat, cover and continue cooking 15 to 20 minutes, until caramelized. Set aside.

In a large pot, combine potatoes, stock and cream and season with salt and pepper. Simmer, stirring gently so not to break potato slices. Cook until barely tender, about 10 minutes.

Use a slotted spoon to transfer a layer of potatoes into a buttered, deep 9x13-inch baking dish. Add enough potato liquid from pot to cover. Sprinkle with Parmesan cheese and add a layer of onions. Repeat until dish is full. ***Important: leave at least 1 inch of rim showing.***

Combine breadcrumbs and asiago cheese, and sprinkle over top. Dab with remaining butter and bake 40 to 50 minutes, until golden brown and bubbly. Let sit 10 to 15 minutes before serving.

Nothing beats fresh breadcrumbs. I make my own with leftover, even slightly stale, bread. I pulse it in the food processor to form crumbs, and then pop the crumbs in plastic freezer bags. When I need breadcrumbs, I open a bag, and toast the breadcrumbs in the oven for a few minutes. Easy.

In our opinion, everything is better with cheese. Our recipe uses Parmesan and asiago, but any of your favorites will work.

# Stuffed Baked Potatoes with Romanesco

Serves 4

Preheat oven to 325°F.

4 russet potatoes
1 tablespoon olive oil
Salt and pepper to taste
¼ pound bacon, diced
2 cups romanesco, cut into small florets
2 tablespoons butter
¼ cup Roquefort cheese, crumbled
¼ cup sour cream

Coat potatoes with oil, salt and pepper, and wrap with foil. Bake 40 to 45 minutes, until tender. Meanwhile, cook bacon in a small sauté pan until crisp. Remove from pan, and sauté romanesco in remaining bacon fat. Season lightly with salt and pepper.
Turn oven to broil.
Unwrap potatoes and cut in half lengthwise. Using a fork, gently mix butter into each potato. Add more salt and pepper if desired. Top with bacon, romanesco and crumbled cheese. Broil potatoes until cheese is melted. Top with sour cream before serving.

*Don't ingest foods made in places where everyone is required to wear a surgical cap.*
*—Michael Pollan*

# March 19
# Lettuce

Mixed Greens with Kohlrabi and
Radishes and Garlic Oregano Vinaigrette

Chicken Livers with Balsamic Vinegar and Goat Cheese

Lettuce Wraps

*E*xtra virgin olive oil (EVOO) is the freshest, healthiest grade of olive oil available. Often compared to pure fruit juice, EVOO is made from olives that are picked and "squeezed" the same day without using heat or chemicals that augment the extraction process or change the nature of the oil.

All olive oils are monounsaturated, but EVOO has the lowest percentage of free fatty acids (less than .5%) and the highest level of antioxidants.

EVOO also contains a naturally occurring non-steroidal anti-inflammatory chemical that functions like ibuprofen.

In a 2010 study, researchers at UC Davis found many imported extra virgin olive oils don't actually qualify as extra virgin by either international or USDA standards. To be sure you're getting authentic extra virgin, look for the California Olive Oil Council's certification seal. You'll be supporting local growers and getting the freshest, highest quality EVOO available.

# Lettuce

## Mixed Greens with Kohlrabi and Radishes and Garlic Oregano Vinaigrette

Serves 4

2 to 3 cups mixed greens
2 kohlrabi, peeled and thinly sliced
1 bunch radishes, sliced
Salt and pepper to taste
¼ cup cheese, your choice

Combine salad ingredients. Toss salad with 2 tablespoons garlic oregano vinaigrette and serve.

### Garlic Oregano Vinaigrette

Makes 2 cups

1½ cups olive oil
½ cup red wine vinegar
¼ to ½ cup fresh or dried oregano (if fresh, slice leaves in half)
½ head garlic, chopped
Salt and pepper to taste

Put all ingredients in a quart jar. Shake well. Keep at room temperature 4 days, until flavors are infused. Shake at least once a day. After 4 days, strain dressing; discard oregano and garlic. Stored in a tightly sealed jar, dressing will keep 3 to 4 weeks in refrigerator.

## Chicken Livers with Balsamic Vinegar and Goat Cheese

Serves 4

2 tablespoons butter
2 onions, julienne
¼ cup balsamic vinegar
Salt and pepper to taste
1 pound chicken livers
2 tablespoons grapeseed oil
2 cups mixed lettuces
4 ounces goat cheese

To make vinegar reduction: In a large sauté pan, cook butter and onions over high heat, stirring frequently. Reduce heat to low, cover and let cook until soft. Increase heat and add vinegar. Simmer until reduced by half. Season to taste with salt and pepper. Set aside.

Salt and pepper livers. Heat oil and sear livers 2½ minutes on all sides. Remove from pan when golden brown.

To assemble, arrange greens on platter, drizzle vinegar reduction over greens, and top with livers and onions. Sprinkle goat cheese on top.

The garlic oregano vinaigrette is an infused salad dressing. If you're making an infused dressing, it's just as easy to make a big batch as it is to make a small amount. Several times a year I make a large jar of garlic oregano vinaigrette. Having homemade salad dressings in the refrigerator simplifies my life.

# Lettuce Wraps

Serves 8

3 kohlrabi, peeled and julienne
6 radishes, thinly sliced
4 carrots, peeled and thinly sliced
1 tablespoon grapeseed oil
3 portabella mushrooms, sliced
Salt and pepper to taste
12 sprigs cilantro
8 large lettuce leaves
Soy sauce (optional)

Place kohlrabi, radishes and carrots in ice water to crisp after slicing.
In a large sauté pan, heat oil and quickly sauté mushrooms. Season lightly with salt and pepper and let cool.
To assemble, place vegetables, mushrooms and cilantro sprigs in a lettuce leaf and fold over into a taco shape. Repeat until all ingredients are used. Drizzle with soy sauce if desired.

Kohlrabi is one of those "what should I do with this?" vegetables. Part of the turnip family, it's also called cabbage turnip, and comes in white and purple varieties. Its crunchy texture and slightly spicy flavor makes a delicious addition to salads or crudités. It tastes sweeter when sautéed or steamed.

# March 26
# Mushrooms

Mushroom Arancini
Mushroom Soup
Purée of Mushroom Soup with Blue Cheese Crostini
Amaranth Cakes with Mushrooms

## Mushroom Arancini

Serves 12 as an appetizer

2 tablespoons butter
1 onion, diced
2 cloves garlic, minced
½ pound mushrooms, diced
Salt and pepper to taste
½ cup white wine
2 cups Arborio rice
4 cups chicken or vegetable stock, heated
½ cup Parmesan cheese, grated
4 ounces mozzarella cheese,
    cut into ½-inch cubes
1 cup flour, seasoned with salt and pepper
2 eggs, beaten
1 cup panko breadcrumbs
2 cups vegetable oil

In a large skillet, heat 1 tablespoon butter. Add onions and garlic, and cook until fragrant. Add mushrooms and continue to cook. Season with salt and pepper. Add wine, and cook until mixture is reduced by half. Add rice and 1½ cups hot stock. Stirring frequently, add more stock, ½ cup at a time as it is absorbed. Continue cooking until rice is tender. Remove from heat and stir in remaining butter and Parmesan cheese. Spread rice mixture (risotto) in a thin layer on a sheet tray. Refrigerate to cool. Take a tablespoon of risotto and a piece of mozzarella, and make a 1-inch ball. Coat rice ball in flour, then egg, then breadcrumbs. Heat oil in a large skillet and fry until golden brown. Serve with marinara sauce.

*Ah, risotto...one of my favorite dishes! Its perfectly cheesy flavor and texture is truly love in a bowl. The Arborio rice used in this dish gives it a uniquely creamy texture. Make a batch of rice for dinner, and then fry up the leftovers for arancini.*

# Mushrooms

## Mushroom Soup

Serves 8 to 12

1 ounce dried organic porcini mushrooms
1 tablespoon olive oil
1 tablespoon butter
1 cup yellow onions, diced
2 garlic cloves, diced
1 pound fresh oyster or crimini mushrooms, diced
1½ cups celery leaves, finely sliced
1 cup Yukon Gold potatoes, peeled and
   diced into ½-inch squares
1 quart turkey or chicken broth
½ teaspoon dried thyme or 1 teaspoon fresh thyme
1 teaspoon dried or fresh sage, finely sliced
1 teaspoon salt
Fresh chives, finely sliced

In a saucepan boil one quart water. Add dried mushrooms to water and soak overnight, or at least two hours. Remove mushrooms from water. Reserve water. Purée mushrooms with ½ cup of soaking water. Set aside.
In a large pot, heat olive oil and butter. Add onions and garlic. Sauté until limp.
Add fresh mushrooms, celery leaves, potatoes, puréed mushrooms, remaining soaking water and broth. Add herbs and salt. Bring to a boil. Immediately reduce heat and simmer 35 to 40 minutes, or until vegetables and mushrooms are easily pierced with a fork. Purée soup with a hand-held blender. To serve, sprinkle fresh chives on top.

## Purée of Mushroom Soup with Blue Cheese Crostini

Serves 6 to 8

Preheat oven to 350°F.

1 tablespoon butter
1 tablespoon olive oil
1 onion, cut into 1-inch pieces
2 cloves garlic, minced
4 portabella mushrooms, gills removed,
   cut into 1-inch pieces
Salt and pepper to taste
2 cups chicken stock
1 cup cream
8 thin slices rustic bread, halved
2 ounces blue cheese
Chives to garnish

In a medium pot, heat butter and oil. Add onions and garlic and cook until fragrant. Add mushrooms, season lightly with salt and pepper, add stock and cream, and bring to a boil. Reduce heat and simmer 25 minutes. Remove from heat. Place soup mixture in blender, careful not to fill blender pitcher more than ⅔ full. Purée until smooth. Continue until all soup is puréed. Check seasoning.
To make crostini, spread bread on sheet tray and toast in oven until golden brown. Sprinkle blue cheese over bread half way through toasting. Set aside when done.
Garnish each serving of soup with blue cheese crostini and chives on the side.

*It's not food if it arrived through the window of your car.* —Michael Pollan

# Amaranth Cakes with Mushrooms

Serves 4 to 6

1 cup amaranth

1½ cups vegetable or chicken stock

¼ cup spring onions, diced

1 teaspoon salt

1 egg

2 tablespoons flour

1 tablespoon marjoram or oregano, chopped

3 tablespoons grapeseed oil

1 pound mushrooms, diced

Salt and pepper to taste

1 clove garlic, minced

½ cup white wine

2 tablespoon butter

1 tablespoon parsley, chopped

1 cup Parmesan cheese, grated

Place amaranth, stock, 2 tablespoons onions and salt in a medium saucepan. Bring to a simmer, cover and reduce heat to very low. Cook about 60 minutes, until all the liquid is absorbed.

Transfer to a mixing bowl and cool. Stir in egg, flour and marjoram (or oregano). Set aside.

Heat 1 tablespoon oil in a large skillet and add mushrooms. Season lightly with salt and pepper and continue to cook until they begin to brown. Add remaining onions and garlic; cook 1 minute and add wine. Continue to cook until wine is reduced by half, and stir in butter and parsley. Reduce heat to keep warm.

To fry cakes, heat remaining oil in a large skillet over medium heat and drop 2 tablespoons of amaranth batter in pan. Flatten with a fork into a pancake shape. After golden brown on both sides, transfer to a paper towel to remove excess oil.

To serve, spoon mushroom mixture on cakes and top with Parmesan cheese.

---

Mushrooms, without fillings or sautéed in butter, are very low in calories. In fact, a cup of sliced mushrooms has just 15 calories. Of course, they're delicious prepared with butter and other rich ingredients, but clearly, the key to keeping mushroom dishes healthy lies more in the sauce than in the mushroom.

*Clockwise from bottom: Grits, Barley, Red Quinoa, Polenta, Pink Rice*

*April 2*

# Grains

Mushroom and Barley Soup

Cous Cous with Mushrooms

Grits with Prawns

Polenta Pound Cake

*Eat foods made from ingredients that you can picture growing in their raw state or growing in nature.* —Michael Pollan

## Mushroom and Barley Soup

Serves 6

3 tablespoons olive oil

1 cup carrots, peeled and diced

2 cups torpedo onions, diced

½ cup celery, diced

1 teaspoon dried thyme leaves

1 pound Shitake mushrooms, thinly sliced

8 cups chicken stock

1 cup barley

Salt and pepper to taste

Heat 2 tablespoons oil in stock pot over medium heat. Add carrots, onions, and celery. Cook until tender, but not browned. Stir in remaining oil, thyme and mushrooms. Continue cooking until mushrooms are soft.

Add 4 cups chicken stock to pot. Cover and simmer 30 minutes.

In a 2-quart sauce pan, place remaining stock and barley. Bring to a boil. Reduce heat and simmer 25 to 30 minutes. Add to soup. Salt and pepper to taste.

# Grains

## Cous Cous with Mushrooms

Serves 8

3 cups stock (chicken or vegetable)
1 ounce dried mushrooms
Salt and pepper to taste
1 tablespoon butter
1 pound fresh mushrooms, quartered
2 cloves garlic, minced
½ onion, minced
¼ cup white wine
1 teaspoon thyme
2 cups cous cous
2 tablespoons parsley or basil, chopped
¼ cup Parmesan cheese, grated
3 tablespoons chives, diced

In a medium saucepan, bring stock and dried mushrooms to a boil, and season lightly with salt and pepper. Reduce heat and gently simmer 45 to 60 minutes. Strain and discard mushrooms; set stock aside.

Heat butter in a large skillet and sauté fresh mushrooms until caramelized. Add garlic and onions and continue to cook until fragrant. Add wine and thyme, and cook 2 minutes. Add 2½ cups reserved mushroom stock and reduce heat to simmer.

Place cous cous in a large, heat-proof bowl, and pour stock mixture over cous cous. Cover with a clean dish towel, and steam 5 to 7 minutes. Fluff with fork. Stir in herbs and season to taste with salt and pepper. Garnish with Parmesan cheese and chives.

# Grits with Prawns

Serves 4

¾ cup grits
Salt and pepper to taste
¼ cup Parmesan cheese, grated
¼ cup butter
2 cloves garlic, minced
1½ pounds prawns, peeled and deveined
½ teaspoon cayenne pepper
1 lemon, juiced
Parmesan cheese, shaved, for garnish

In a medium pot, bring 3 cups water to a boil, stir in grits and season lightly with salt and pepper. Reduce heat to low and continue cooking, stirring frequently, until grains are tender and liquid is almost absorbed.
Remove from heat, stir in Parmesan and 2 tablespoons butter. Cover to keep warm.
In a large sauté pan, heat remaining butter and cook garlic until fragrant. Add prawns, season with salt, pepper and cayenne, and continue to sauté until just cooked through. Toss with lemon juice.
To serve, place grits in a large bowl, top with prawns and pan jus. Garnish with shaved Parmesan.

# Polenta Pound Cake

Serves 10 to 12

Preheat oven to 350°F.

3¼ cups flour
1 cup polenta
1 teaspoon baking powder
1 teaspoon salt
1 pound butter, room temperature
2⅓ cups sugar
9 eggs
2 tablespoons orange zest
¾ cup sour cream

Sift together flour, polenta, baking powder and salt. Set aside.
In a mixer, cream butter and sugar until fluffy, about 5 minutes. Add eggs, one at a time, and then add dry ingredients in batches. Fold in zest and sour cream until well combined, careful not to over mix.
Spoon into a buttered Bundt pan, and bake 70 minutes, or until toothpick comes out clean.

# Carrots

Carrot Soup with Baharat-Spiced Croutons
Red Wine Stew
Beer-Braised Rabbit with Pasta and Baby Carrots
Braised Short Ribs

Orange, yellow, red, white and purple! We're talking about carrots, not the rainbow. Not only colorful, carrots are also sweet and full of beta-carotene, which provides vitamin A.

Carrots are one of the most adaptable vegetables. Who doesn't remember snacking on a bag of baby carrots while sitting by a lake, on a hike, or in the lunch your mom packed? They're also great for flavoring stews, broths and soups. And no other vegetable can beat that gorgeous orange color paired with broccoli, romanesco or green beans.

In the springtime, select carrots with the tops on. The bright green leaves mean the carrots were just picked and will easily keep for a couple weeks in the bottom drawer of the refrigerator. Don't throw away the tops. Tie them together and toss them in the pot when making a broth or stew.

# Carrots

## Carrot Soup with Baharat-Spiced Croutons

Serves 6

2 tablespoons olive oil or butter
1 cup onions, chopped
2 cloves garlic, diced
4 cups water
2 pounds organic carrots, peeled and thinly sliced
1 teaspoon salt
½ teaspoon baharat spice

Place oil in a soup pan; add onions and garlic. Sauté until soft. Add water, carrots and salt. Simmer until carrots are soft. Use a hand blender to purée carrot mixture. Add baharat and taste; add more in ½ teaspoon increments if desired. Garnish with baharat-spiced croutons.

### Baharat-Spiced Croutons
Preheat oven to 375°F.

1 tablespoon butter, melted
½ loaf ciabatta bread, crusts removed, bread sliced into ½-inch cubes
½ to 1 teaspoon baharat spice
Salt and pepper to taste

Combine butter and bread cubes. Add ½ teaspoon baharat. Add more in ½ teaspoon increments if desired. Salt and pepper to taste. Roast on a sheet tray 8 minutes, until brown and crispy.

# Red Wine Stew

Serves 6

1 pound beef stew meat, cut into 1-inch cubes
Salt and pepper to taste
½ cup all purpose flour
3 tablespoons grapeseed oil
½ pound mushrooms, halved
1 cup onions, diced
2 cloves garlic, diced
2 cups red wine
4 cups beef stock
1 bay leaf
2 cups carrots, cut ½-inch thick
1 tablespoon each parsley and thyme, chopped

Season beef with salt and pepper and lightly coat in flour.

In a large pot, heat oil. Sear beef on all sides and remove from pot. Add more oil if necessary and sauté mushrooms until slightly browned. Add onions and garlic and continue to cook until fragrant. Add red wine; cook 2 to 3 minutes and add meat, stock and bay leaf. Bring to a boil. Reduce heat, and simmer until meat is tender, about 1 hour. Add carrots and continue to simmer 10 to 15 minutes. Stir in herbs and season to taste with salt and pepper.

# Carrots

## Beer-Braised Rabbit with Pasta and Baby Carrots

Serves 6

Preheat oven to 325°F.

2 rabbits, cut into 6 pieces each

Salt and pepper to taste

1 teaspoon bay seasoning

1 tablespoon grapeseed oil

1½ cups golden ale (we used Blue Moon)

10 cloves garlic, peeled and smashed

4 carrots, peeled and halved

4 stalks celery, halved

1 onion, peeled and halved

2 bunches baby carrots

1 pound black pepper and garlic pasta

2 tablespoons parsley, chopped

Season rabbit with salt, pepper and bay seasoning. In a large sauté pan, heat oil and sear rabbit over high heat on both sides, about 2

minutes. Remove from pan and place in a large baking dish with beer, garlic, carrot halves, celery and onions. Marinate 1 hour.

Cover and roast 1 hour. When meat is tender, remove from dish and cool. Remove meat from bones. Set aside. Discard vegetables and bones. Strain and reduce cooking liquid by half. Add baby carrots and cook 2 minutes.

Meanwhile, cook pasta in boiling salted water until tender.

Toss pasta with rabbit meat and baby carrots, and enough braising liquid to coat. Garnish with chopped parsley.

# Braised Short Ribs

Serves 6

Preheat oven to 325°F.

3 to 4 racks beef short ribs, cut into 1-rib pieces
1 bunch carrots, peeled and large diced
1 bottle red wine
Salt and pepper
2 tablespoons oil
1 teaspoon bay seasoning
2 tablespoons butter
Salt and pepper to taste

Place ribs in a large bowl with carrots and wine. Cover and refrigerate 8 to 12 hours.
Remove ribs and dry with a paper towel. Season ribs with salt and pepper.
In a large oven proof pan, heat oil. Sear ribs on both sides. Add marinating liquid, including carrots, and bay seasoning. Cover with foil and bake 1½ to 2 hours, until tender. Cool in jus. Remove ribs, and strain jus into a medium saucepan. Bring to a boil and reduce by one half. Reduce heat to low, stir in butter and season to taste with salt and pepper. Pour finished jus over ribs and serve.

*April 16*

# Eggs

Open-Faced Egg Salad Sandwich

Crostini with Smoked Salmon and Hard-Boiled Egg

Potato Salad

Croque Madame

Sheep Milk Tapioca Cream Pudding

*H*aving an "egg lady" is one of the joys of living the good and tasty life, especially when the egg lady gets her eggs from free-range, walk-around chickens with their feet on the ground. From my point of view, the ingredients for great meals come from food grown in the ground or as close to the ground as possible. That makes free-range chicken eggs high quality eggs.

In high quality eggs both the white and the yolk stand up higher and the whites spread less than in low quality eggs. Egg shell color has nothing to do with taste or nutritive value. Eggs are an excellent source of protein and vitamins A and D. Most recipes are based on large size eggs.

# Eggs

## Open-Faced Egg Salad Sandwich

Serves 4

10 eggs
1 tablespoon white vinegar
¼ cup mayonnaise
½ cup celery, diced
Truffle salt (optional)
Salt and pepper to taste
½ cup celery leaves
4 slices artisan bread, about 1 inch thick

Place eggs in a small pan with vinegar and cover with water. Bring to a boil, cover, turn off heat and let sit 10 minutes. Run under cold water to cool. If eggs are farm fresh, crack the shell slightly while still warm to make peeling easier. Peel and dice eggs, and place in a medium bowl with mayonnaise, celery and seasoning. Mix to combine.
Serve egg salad over a bed of celery leaves on artisan bread.

*Eat slowly.    —Michael Pollan.*

## Crostini with Smoked Salmon and Hard-Boiled Egg

Serves 4

Preheat oven to 375°F.

5 to 6 quail eggs
1 teaspoon white vinegar
8 slices artisan bread
2 to 3 tablespoons olive oil
¼ cup cream cheese
8 slices smoked salmon
1 tablespoon capers
Sea salt and pepper to taste

Place eggs in a small pot with vinegar and just enough water to cover. Bring to a boil, cover and turn off heat. Let stand 8 minutes. Drain from hot water, gently crack and run eggs under cold water 2 minutes to cool. Carefully peel and slice lengthwise. Set aside.
Brush bread with oil and toast in oven until golden brown, 10 to 12 minutes.
Spread a thin layer of cream cheese and place a piece of salmon on each crostini, top with egg and capers. Drizzle with olive oil, sea salt and pepper.

> If your grocery store doesn't sell quail eggs, you can substitute another type of small egg, such as pullet or bantam eggs.

# Potato Salad

Serves 6

1½ pounds Yukon Gold potatoes, peeled

1 cup mayonnaise, or ½ cup
  mayonnaise and ½ cup Greek yogurt

⅓ cup sweet relish

2 tablespoons Worcestershire sauce

1 teaspoon salt

½ teaspoon pepper

1 tablespoon Dijon mustard

2 tablespoons Italian parsley, finely diced

3 eggs, hard boiled and diced

Salt and pepper to taste

1 cup celery, finely diced

1 cup Torpedo onions, finely diced

Hungarian paprika

2 to 3 parsley stems

Cook potatoes in salted water until fork tender. Drain and let cool. Set aside.

Meanwhile, blend mayonnaise, relish, Worcestershire sauce, salt, pepper, Dijon mustard and parsley. Set aside.

Slice potatoes into ½-inch square cubes; add diced eggs. Pour mayonnaise mixture over potatoes and carefully blend. Add salt and pepper to taste.

Before serving check consistency of salad. Add 1 tablespoon half and half or whole milk if needed to moisturize potatoes. Gently stir in celery and onions.

Cover salad and place in refrigerator, at least 6 hours or overnight.

To serve, sprinkle lightly with paprika and garnish with parsley stems.

## Croque Madame

Serves 4

Preheat oven to 250°F.

8 slices rustic bread
3 tablespoons butter (for bread)
4 ounces aged cheddar cheese, thinly sliced
2 ounces ham, thinly sliced
1 jar blood orange marmalade
1 tablespoon butter
8 eggs
Salt and pepper to taste

Spread butter on one side of each piece of bread. Lay four pieces, butter side down, in a hot pan and add a layer of cheese and ham to each. Spread marmalade on non–buttered side of remaining bread and place on top, marmalade side down.

Toast both sides of sandwich until golden brown and cheese is melted. Remove from pan. Place in a warm oven.

In the same pan, heat 1 tablespoon butter, and baste eggs until cooked to desired doneness.

Cut sandwiches in half and place 1 egg on top of each half. Serve immediately.

> Try basting eggs for the perfect soft-yolk fried egg. In a small cast-iron skillet, melt a small amount of butter. Place an egg or two in the pan, immediately cover and lower heat. After a minute or two peek at the egg; it fries quickly and slips easily onto a plate. No more broken egg yolks while flipping over-easy eggs.

# Sheep Milk Tapioca Cream Pudding

Serves 4 to 6

1 egg yolk
6 tablespoons sugar
3 tablespoons quick-cooking tapioca
1½ cups sheep milk
½ cup whole milk
2 egg whites
1 teaspoon vanilla

Mix egg yolk, 3 tablespoons sugar, tapioca and milk in a medium saucepan. Let stand 5 minutes. Beat egg whites in a medium bowl with electric mixer at high speed until foamy. Gradually add remaining sugar, beating until soft peaks form. Set aside.

Cook tapioca mixture on medium heat, stirring constantly, until mixture comes to a full boil (a boil that doesn't stop bubbling when stirred).

Remove from heat. Quickly fold in egg white mixture until well blended. Stir in vanilla. Cool for 20 minutes. Serve warm or chilled. Serve with fruit topping. Try raspberries, strawberries or a cooked rhubarb and blackberry sauce.

> Sheep's milk is a treat. Because of its high calorie count, you won't want to drink it every day. The milk is delicious in puddings and ice cream. It's also a good source of protein, riboflavin, vitamin B-12, and phosphorus. Enjoy it on special occasions.

*April 23*

# Herbs

Debbie's Mojitos

Chicken Wraps with Asparagus, Lemon and Herbs

Pork Meatballs with Apricot Chutney

Rosemary Roasted Chicken

Green Rice

It's a luxury to have fresh herbs growing just outside the door for snipping and adding to dishes. Herbs are among the easiest plants to grow. They're seldom bothered by pests or diseases. Most are sun-worshippers that get more aromatic and tastier when ignored. They disdain fertilizer and respond well to constant harvesting. Further, they require precious little water. Even a tiny herb garden – with the vegetables, in hanging baskets, among the flowers and roses, on the windowsill – can produce more fresh herbs than a family can use.

The best place to plant them is where you'll walk by them. I love herbs planted among the perennials and shrubs along the walkway to my front door because I can rub my hand across them and inhale their amazing aroma every time I walk by. I have a pot of chives on the deck, and a hanging basket filled with sage, parsley and oregano near the back door. Sure, they might outgrow the pot by the end of the season, but meanwhile they're close at hand if I need a few sprigs to season a meal or as a decorative garnish.

You might ask why grow herbs when they're so easy to buy, fresh or dried, at the grocery store. If you've ever tasted and dried your own basil or parsley flakes, or made pesto with basil picked just minutes before, you'll never want to buy supermarket packaged herbs again.

# Herbs

## Debbie's Mojitos

Serves 1

*Thanks to Debbie Dutra for this recipe.*

½ lime, cut in half
Hand full of mint leaves
1 tablespoon simple syrup (recipe below)
Shaved or crushed ice
Soda water, plain or lime flavored
Lime wedges and mint leaves for garnish

In a large, sturdy glass, muddle the lime quarters; take your time and really get a good amount of juice and zest from the lime. Add mint and muddle the mixture together again. Add simple syrup and muddle one more time.
Add crushed ice to within 1 inch of top of glass.
Top with soda water. Garnish with a wedge of lime and mint leaves.
If you enjoy the taste of rum, add rum before the ice and soda water.

### Simple Syrup
Makes one quart

2 cups water
1 cup sugar
½ cup lemon juice
Zest from one whole lemon or lime or both

Place all ingredients in two quart sauce pan.
Bring to a boil and stir until sugar is dissolved.
Cool and transfer to a quart jar. Lasts 1 month in refrigerator.

I keep a small container of simple syrup in the refrigerator. It's the easy way to sweeten frozen or fresh fruit, ice tea or lemonade. For example, if strawberries are in season, steep the berries in the syrup, strain the syrup and voila you have strawberry-flavored sweetener. Try peaches, blackberries or mandarins for the same result.

# Chicken Wraps with Asparagus, Lemon and Herbs

Serves 4

Preheat oven to 375°F.

1 bunch asparagus, bottoms trimmed
1 tablespoon olive oil
Salt and pepper to taste
4 large tortillas
8 ounces Gina Marie cream cheese
1 tablespoon tarragon, chopped
2 lemons, zested
2 cups cooked chicken, shredded

Season asparagus with oil, salt and pepper and roast on a sheet tray until just tender, 8 to 12 minutes. Remove from oven and set aside.

Combine cream cheese, tarragon and lemon zest; season to taste with salt and pepper.
If tortillas are not pliable, warm in a dry fry pan on stove top 15 to 25 seconds. Spread cream cheese on half of tortilla, arrange asparagus and chicken on other half. Roll up to and seal edge with a bit more cream cheese. To serve, cut in half, or slice for appetizers.

# Herbs

## Pork Meatballs with Apricot Chutney

Serves 4

Preheat oven to 325°F.

1 tablespoon olive oil
½ onion, minced
1 clove garlic, minced
1 pound ground pork
1 teaspoon oregano, chopped
1 tablespoon basil, chopped
¼ cup ricotta cheese
1 egg, beaten
½ cup panko breadcrumbs
Salt and pepper to taste
2 tablespoons grapeseed oil
2 cups chicken stock

Heat olive oil in large pan, add onions and garlic, and cook until fragrant. Remove from heat and place in a large bowl.
Add meat, herbs, ricotta, egg and breadcrumbs; season lightly with salt and pepper. When well combined, cook a small portion of meat to check seasoning.
Form meat mixture into 1-inch balls.
Heat grapeseed oil in a large oven-proof pan and sear meatballs on all sides. Don't overcrowd pan; cook in batches if necessary.
Return all meatballs to pan. Add stock, bring to a rolling simmer, cover and place in the oven. Bake 25 to 35 minutes.
To serve, remove meatballs from stock. Serve with apricot chutney.

### Apricot Chutney

1 tablespoon olive oil
¼ onion, minced
3 cups apricots, pitted and quartered
2 teaspoons oregano, chopped
¼ teaspoon thyme leaves
1 tablespoon basil, chopped
½ cup chicken stock
¼ teaspoon chili flakes
Salt and pepper to taste

In a medium pot, heat oil and cook onions until fragrant. Add remaining ingredients. Simmer 15 to 20 minutes.

# Rosemary Roasted Chicken

Serves 4 to 6

*This recipe was inspired by Joel Salatin.*

Preheat oven to 350°F.

1 whole chicken, 3 to 4 pounds
1 lemon, sliced
12 to 15 rosemary branches, or enough to line
   edge of roasting pan
1 tablespoon butter or olive oil
Salt and pepper

Stuff chicken with 3 or 4 rosemary branches and lemon slices. Rub skin with butter or oil and season with salt and pepper.

Place remaining branches in bottom of a large baking pan; place a few on the side of the chicken.

Place chicken on rosemary. Roast 1 to 1½ hours, until the legs are loose and the juices flow clear. Here's where the fun begins: Take the pan with the chicken outside, place on a concrete path, the lawn, or a brick or cement patio (away from the house). Use a match to light fire to one of the rosemary sprigs. The fire will quickly move around the pan. Let the fire die out, then place chicken on a platter and take inside. Remove legs and thighs, and carve breast.

Sounds quirky, but everyone loves to watch the flaming chicken.

# Green Rice

Serves 6

1½ pounds tomatillos, husks removed, quartered
½ cup water
1 tablespoon jalapeno, minced
1 clove garlic, minced
Salt and pepper to taste
1¼ cups long grain brown rice
¼ cup cilantro, chopped

Purée tomatillos, water, jalapeno and garlic until smooth. Add salt and pepper to taste.

Transfer 2½ cups purée to a medium saucepan, and bring to a boil. Stir in rice. Reduce heat, cover and simmer 45 minutes, until rice is tender and liquid is absorbed. Fluff with a fork and fold in cilantro.

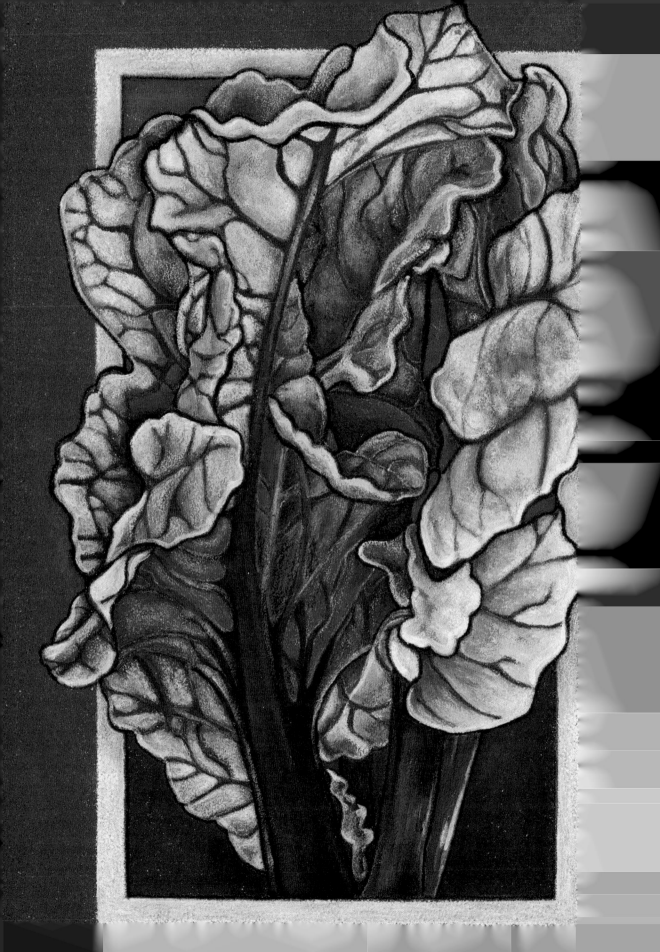

# Red Chard and Rhubarb

Swiss Chard Soup

Fried Chard Stems with Blue Cheese Love

Sautéed Chard with Currants

Rhubarb and Raspberry Pie

*B*efore we lift a fork to our mouths, we've already tasted the food with our eyes. That's why Laura and I incorporate lots of color into a meal. I liken it to choreographing a dance on the plate. Color makes the plate visually exciting, leads your eye across the whole "stage" and creates harmony. It also makes for a nutritionally balanced meal. You don't need to memorize what each color means. Just keep your plates colorful and let Nature do the work for you.

It's no surprise that people new to farmers markets most often comment on the brilliant colors of the produce. Farmers markets look as though a paint box spilled down on them from the heavens. These marvelous colors are Nature's way of making the foods that are best for you the most attractive. The brighter and more varied the colors of our food, the richer the food in nutritional value. For example, dark leafy greens like spinach and kale are loaded with B vitamins, iron, calcium and magnesium. Orange and yellow veggies are a valuable source of vitamin A, which bolsters the immune system and improves eyesight. Red, blue and purple foods, such as blueberries, cherries, beets and eggplant, are high in antioxidants.

# Red Chard & Rhubarb

## Swiss Chard Soup

Serves 4

*Thanks to Lynn Archer for the basic recipe.*

2 tablespoons olive oil

2 cloves garlic, diced

2 stalks celery, chopped

2 carrots, chopped

1 bunch chard leaves, coarsely chopped

3 cups stock

2 potatoes, peeled, halved, and thinly sliced

¼ pound penne pasta

Salt and pepper to taste

½ cup Parmesan cheese, grated

In a large pot, heat oil and lightly sauté garlic, celery and carrots. Add chard leaves and sauté 2 to 3 minutes. Add stock and potatoes and bring to a boil. Add pasta, reduce heat to simmer and cook 10 to 15 minutes, until pasta is tender. Season to taste with salt and pepper. Garnish with cheese.

# Fried Chard Stems with Blue Cheese Love

Serves 8

*This recipe was inspired by Lynn Archer.*

¼ cup flour
¼ cup Parmesan cheese, grated
Salt and pepper to taste
1 egg, beaten
2 bunches young chard stems, cleaned,
    cut into 4-inch pieces
1 tablespoon butter
1 tablespoon olive oil

Combine flour, Parmesan, salt and pepper in a medium bowl. In another bowl, place beaten egg. Dip each stem in egg, then flour mixture.
Heat butter and oil in a large skillet, and fry chard stems until golden brown on both sides, 4 to 7 minutes.

Place on a paper towel to dry, and season with salt and pepper.
Serve warm with Blue Cheese Love.

## Blue Cheese Love

1 cup cream
2 ounces Pt. Reyes blue cheese
Salt and pepper to taste

In a small saucepan, heat cream and reduce by one half. Turn off heat, stir in cheese and season to taste with salt and pepper.

*www.theartofrealfood.com*

# Red Chard & Rhubarb

## Sautéed Chard with Currants

Serves 4

2 bunches chard, stems sliced in 1-inch pieces,
  leaves coarsely chopped

1 tablespoon butter

1 tablespoon olive oil

1 tablespoon shallots, minced

1 clove garlic, minced

3 tablespoons dried currants

3 tablespoons pine nuts, toasted

Salt and pepper to taste

Blanch chard stems in a small pot of boiling, salted water, about 20 seconds. Immediately transfer to a bowl of ice water. Cool, drain and set aside.

In a large sauté pan, heat butter and oil. Add shallots and garlic, and cook until fragrant. Add chard leaves and continue to cook until wilted. Add currants, pine nuts and chard stems and season to taste with salt and pepper.

ᶜᵘ꙳ᵒ Use the same recipe for other rhubarb pies, replacing the raspberries with blackberries, boysenberries, marionberries, olallieberries or strawberries. All are delicious during the lengthy rhubarb season.

# Rhubarb and Raspberry Pie

Serves 8

Preheat oven to 400°F.

### Two crust pie dough for 9-inch pie

¼ cup vegetable shortening
¼ cup cold butter
1½ cups all purpose flour
½ teaspoon salt
¼ cup cold water
½ teaspoon cinnamon
½ teaspoon sugar (mix with cinnamon)
1 teaspoon Demerara sugar (optional)

Use a pie dough cutter to blend shortening, butter, flour and salt to cornmeal stage. Slowly add cold water, mixing with a fork, until dough comes together. Add more water if necessary. Form into a ball, cover and chill at least 2 hours before rolling out.

Cut the dough ball into two pieces, one slightly larger than the other. Roll out dough on a floured surface until ⅛-inch thick. Make dough 10 inches for bottom, and 9 inches for top.

Place filling in the shell. Apply top crust. Trim, roll and crimp edges. Score the dough 6 or 7 places to allow air to vent. Sprinkle top with cinnamon sugar mixture, then Demerara.

### Filling

3 cups rhubarb, sliced
2 cups frozen raspberries
1 cup sugar
¼ cup orange or tangelo juice
2 teaspoons orange zest
½ teaspoon salt
⅓ cup tapioca flour
1 tablespoon cold butter

In a large bowl combine all ingredients except butter. Stir gently and let stand for 20 minutes. Stir again and pour mixture into pie pan lined with crust. Put small dabs of butter over filling. Cover filling with remaining piece of dough. Bake 50 to 60 minutes. Cool before slicing and serving.

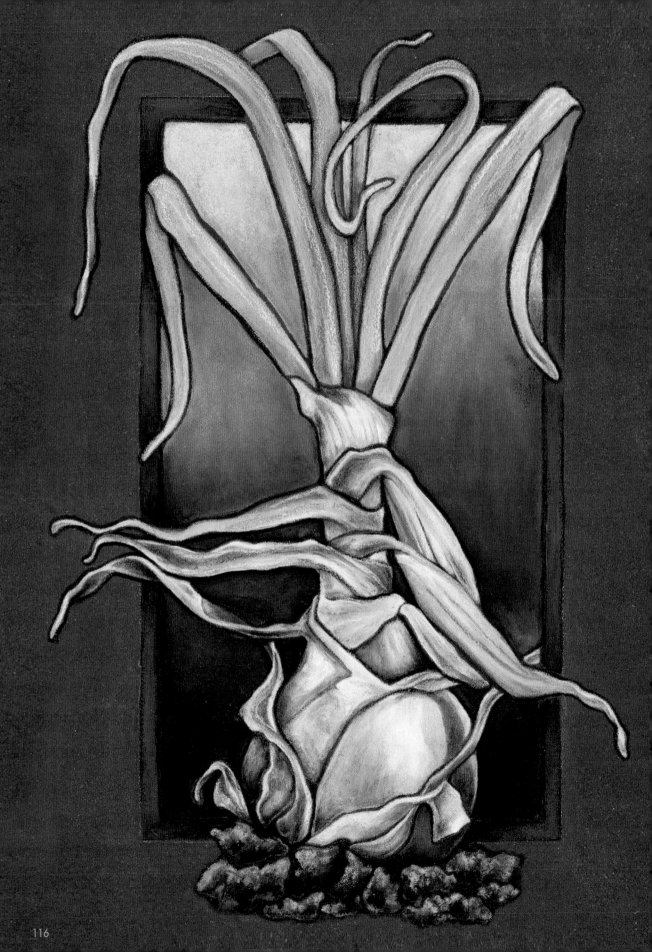

# Onions

Stacked Potatoes and Placer Sweet Onions
Asparagus, Mushroom and Spring Onion Pasta
Savory Crepes with Chicken
Roasted Pork Tenderloin with Placer Sweet Onions and Flageolet Beans

Onions: the king of globe vegetables. Luckily our farmers market features several types of green onions (scallions) and dry onions.

Spring onions are among the best! You know spring has finally arrived when one or two growers bring freshly picked spring onions to the market. They're perfect in stir fries and spring salads, and useful as a colorful garnish.

Among other onion varieties, one of our favorites is the Placer Sweet. They're large, pale yellow onions, very juicy with a sweet taste. Another favorite is the Walla Walla, named after a city in Washington. Walla Wallas show up on market tables between June and September.

Available year-round, dried onions include white or yellow Bermuda onions, and red or Italian onions. Depending on where they're grown and when they are picked, dried onions are mildly pungent to quite sharp in taste.

Store onions in a cool, dry place in a natural fiber or wire basket, and they'll keep for several months.

*Serve the vegetables first.* –Michael Pollan

117

# Onions

This recipe was inspired by a container of leftover mashed potatoes I found in the refrigerator. Hmmm. I didn't want the potatoes to go to waste, so I wondered what I could make that would be a little different. I rummaged through the fridge, found bacon and cheese, looked on the counter and saw Placer Sweet onions, and suddenly a new recipe began to take shape. You can do the same, of course, with a bit of imagination and leftovers.

## Stacked Potatoes and Placer Sweet Onions

Serves 6

Preheat oven to broil.

3 pounds German Butterball potatoes, peeled and cut into uniform size pieces

½ cup half and half

3 tablespoons butter

Salt and pepper to taste

¾ pound bacon, diced

2 Placer Sweet onions, peeled, sliced into ¾-inch thick round slices

Salt and pepper to taste

4 ounces Parmesan cheese, grated

Cook potatoes in salted water until fork tender. Drain and let dry.

In a small saucepan, heat half and half until scalded. Pass potatoes through a mill with butter. Add half and half to desired texture. Add salt and pepper to taste. Set aside.

Cook bacon in a large sauté pan until crisp. Remove from pan, and set aside. Leave bacon fat in pan.

In the same pan, cook onion slices until slightly caramelized on each side. Add salt and pepper to taste.

Remove onion slices from pan and place on a sheet tray. Top each slice with about ½ cup mashed potatoes and generously sprinkle with cheese. Broil until cheese is melted and slightly browned. Top with bacon.

# Asparagus, Mushroom and Spring Onion Pasta

Serves 4

½ cup fava beans, shucked
2 tablespoons olive oil
½ cup spring onions, diced
2 cloves garlic, minced
2 cups mushrooms, halved
1 cup asparagus, cut into 1-inch pieces
½ cup snap peas
1 lemon, juiced
1 tablespoon butter
Salt and pepper to taste
5 ounces whole grain linguini
¼ cup Parmesan cheese
3 tablespoons parsley, chopped

Blanch shucked fava beans by cooking in salted, boiling water for 30 seconds. Remove; cool in ice water. Peel and set aside.

In a large sauté pan, heat oil and cook onions and garlic until fragrant. Add mushrooms and continue to cook until tender. Add asparagus, cook until fork tender. Add peas and fava beans. Add lemon juice and butter. Add salt and pepper to taste.

Cook pasta in boiling salted water. Drain.

Toss vegetables with pasta, Parmesan and parsley before serving.

# Onions

## Savory Crepes with Chicken

Serves 4

2 eggs, lightly beaten
⅔ cup whole milk
1 tablespoon butter, melted
½ cup all purpose flour
1 teaspoon white sugar
Dash salt
1 tablespoon grapeseed oil

Whisk eggs, milk, butter, flour, sugar and salt until blended.

Heat crepe pan over medium heat. Add fine covering of oil. Spoon a scant ¼ cup of crepe batter into pan; tilt pan to totally cover bottom with batter. Cook on medium heat until golden. Turn crepe over and cook another 30 to 45 seconds. Crepes can be made ahead and layered between parchment paper.

## Chicken Filling

1 tablespoon butter
1 cup mushrooms, diced
1 tablespoon shallots, diced
1 teaspoon all purpose flour
½ cup chicken stock
½ cup half and half
1 tablespoon tarragon, chopped
2 cups cooked chicken, diced
Salt and pepper to taste
Basil leaves, chiffonade

In a medium saucepan, heat butter and cook mushrooms until softened. Add shallots and cook until fragrant. Stir in flour and then stock. Bring to a boil, stirring constantly, and reduce heat to simmer.

Stir in half and half and tarragon, then cooked chicken. Season to taste with salt and pepper.

To serve, fill warm crepes with chicken mixture, and garnish with basil.

# Roasted Pork Tenderloin with Placer Sweet Onions and Flageolet Beans

Serves 6 to 8

Preheat oven to 350°F.

1 pound flageolet beans
2 to 3 sprigs each thyme, rosemary and parsley
¼ cup parsley, chopped
2 tablespoons butter
2 large Placer Sweet onions, julienne
Salt and pepper to taste
2 cloves garlic
2 tablespoons grapeseed oil
1½ to 2 pounds pork tenderloin

In a large pot, cover beans with water, at least 1½ inches above beans. Add herb sprigs and bring to a boil over medium heat. Cover and turn down to simmer 1 to 1½ hours. When beans are tender, drain excess water and discard herbs. Stir in parsley and season to taste with salt and pepper. Set aside.

In a large oven-proof pan, heat butter over medium high heat and add onions. Add salt and pepper to taste. Continue to cook, stirring occasionally, until they begin to caramelize. Reduce heat slightly, cover and continue cooking until light golden brown, about 10 minutes. Add garlic halfway through. Remove from pan and set aside.

In the same pan, heat oil. Season pork with salt and pepper, and sear on all sides. Add onions back to pan and finish in oven, 15 to 25 minutes. To serve, place beans on a large platter. Slice pork, arrange on beans, and top with onions.

*May 14*

# Strawberries

Finnish Pancake
Green Leaf Salad with Strawberries and Red Wine Vinaigrette
Strawberry Rhubarb Sauce
Strawberry Fruit Fool

Serve up a bowl of sliced strawberries, sprinkle lightly with sugar and you have a healthy, light dessert.

Strawberries, raspberries, blackberries, blueberries. Is there anything more delectable than a berry? Naturally sweet and bursting with flavor, these summer gems are often called Nature's candy—but don't let that moniker mislead you. Berries are high in fiber and loaded with vitamins and minerals. For example, a single cup of strawberries contains more vitamin C than an orange. Strawberries are also an excellent source of B vitamins, folic acid, manganese, magnesium, potassium and even Omega-3 fatty acids. All these nutritional goodies for only 43 calories per cup!

# Strawberries

## Finnish Pancake

Serves 2

Preheat oven to 425°F.

¼ cup butter, melted
2 eggs, slightly beaten
2 tablespoons honey
¼ teaspoon salt
1¼ cups whole milk, or equal
    parts milk and half and half
½ cup flour
½ teaspoon vanilla
1 tablespoon powdered sugar

In a large bowl blend 2 tablespoons butter, eggs, honey, salt, milk and flour and vanilla. Let mixture rest 5 to 10 minutes.

In 9-inch glass pie dish, place remaining butter. Make sure surface is totally covered.

Pour batter into dish and place on center rack of oven. Bake 18 to 20 minutes.

Remove and sprinkle with light dusting of powdered sugar.

To serve: Top with crème fraîche, sour cream, or fresh fruit lightly sugared.

The pancake grows as it bakes; it's fun to let everyone take a peek immediately before removing it from the oven.

Slice the pancake at the table and place a piece on each plate. Pass around a big bowl of fresh in-season fruit: strawberries, raspberries, blackberries, blueberries, sliced peaches (separately or blended). Top with a spoon of crème fraîche or sour cream. Remember, however, pancake flavor will vary depending on your choice of honey. Orange blossom honey is particularly tasty.

Make Mother's Day breakfast extra special by serving these pancake wedges with a slice of ham or rashers of bacon.

# Green Leaf Salad with Strawberries and Red Wine Vinaigrette

Serves 4

1 head green leaf lettuce, torn into pieces
1 pint strawberries, sliced
1 orange, segmented, reserve juice
¼ cup blue cheese, crumbled

## Red Wine Vinaigrette

2 tablespoons red wine vinegar
¼ cup olive oil
Juice from orange segments
Salt and pepper to taste

Combine salad ingredients. In a separate bowl, whisk together red wine vinegar, olive oil and juice from orange segments. Season to taste with salt and pepper. Toss with salad and serve immediately.

# Strawberry Rhubarb Sauce

Makes 4 cups

½ orange or tangelo, zest and juice
2 cups rhubarb, cut into ½-inch slices
⅓ cup brown sugar
2 cups strawberries, sliced
½ teaspoon vanilla
Crème fraîche

Place juice, rhubarb and brown sugar in a 2-quart sauce pan. Cover pan. Bring to a boil. Immediately reduce heat and simmer 5 minutes. Add zest and gently stir.
Spoon strawberries on top of rhubarb and cover pan; gently simmer 2 minutes.
Turn off heat, leave pan covered until cool. Refrigerate.
Serve in small sauce dishes with a dollop of crème fraîche.

# Strawberry Fruit Fool

Serves 6 to 8

2 baskets strawberries
1 tablespoon sugar
1 cup heavy cream
½ teaspoon vanilla
Mint leaves

Set aside half a basket of smallest strawberries for garnish; purée remaining strawberries with 1 teaspoon sugar. Set aside.
Whip cream and add 2 teaspoons sugar. When almost done, add vanilla and continue to whip until done.
Gently fold puréed strawberries into whipped cream leaving a few white streaks. Pour into glass dishes or stemmed wine glasses. Chill.
To serve, garnish with small berries and a mint leaf.

# May 21

# Blueberries

Mac n' Cheese

Mini Cheesecakes with Blueberries and Raspberries

Blueberry Kuchen

Lemon and Blueberry Tea Cake

ippocrates, the Ancient Greek physician who is called the Father of Medicine, once said, "Let food be thy medicine and let thy medicine be thy food."

I'm convinced he was talking about berries. As a family of fruits, berries are especially high in antioxidants, which are most simply described as rust protection for the body. In the same way you can extend the life of metal objects with protective coatings, the body uses antioxidants to protect and preserve its cells. In this way, antioxidants help slow the aging process and ward off age-related ailments such as heart disease, arthritis and dementia.

# Blueberries

## Mac n' Cheese

Serves 8

Preheat oven to 375°F.

1 tablespoon butter
1 tablespoon flour
4 cups milk
5 cups cheddar cheese, grated
Salt and pepper to taste
1 pound whole wheat pasta (macaroni or penne)
1 cup panko breadcrumbs
1 tablespoon butter, cut into small pieces
Salt and pepper to taste
½ cup bacon, diced and cooked

In a medium saucepan, heat 1 tablespoon butter. Whisk in flour and cook over low heat, 2 to 3 minutes. Stir in milk, bring to a boil, and reduce heat to gently simmer 15 to 20 minutes. Remove from heat, stir in cheese and season to taste with salt and pepper. Set aside.

You may be wondering why a recipe for macaroni and cheese is in the blueberry section. Well, we really wanted to include a great macaroni and cheese recipe, but had no place to put it. We'd already included a bowl of snap peas on the side, but decided something with blueberries would be the perfect foil for the macaroni dish. Start with a green salad topped with a handful of blueberries, a sprinkling of chopped pecans, and a sweet and sour dressing. Finish the meal with the blueberry kuchen or tea cake. Perfect.

Cook pasta per instructions and drain completely.
In a casserole dish, combine pasta and cheddar sauce. Top with breadcrumbs and dabs of butter. Bake 20 to 30 minutes, until golden brown and bubbly. Garnish with bacon.

# Mini Cheesecakes with Blueberries and Raspberries

Makes 50 mini cakes

Preheat oven to 350°F.

## Graham cracker crust
1¼ cups graham cracker crumbs
2 tablespoons sugar
½ cup butter, melted

Blend all ingredients with a fork, place a heaping teaspoon into each mini cup, and gently press down.

## Filling
1 pound Gina Marie cream cheese
2 large eggs
1 teaspoon vanilla
½ cup sugar

Blend ingredients and beat 3 to 4 minutes. Spoon filling into cups with a teaspoon.
Bake 9 or 10 minutes, until tops begin to crack.
Freeze on a cookie sheet, then transfer to airtight container to store. Cakes will keep up to a month.
To serve, defrost cakes 10 minutes, top with a blueberry (or frozen blackberry) and a couple of raspberries.
To save time if you're going to serve all 50 at once, a quick and tasty alternative to putting berries on each mini cheesecake is to blend 1 cup mandarin marmalade with ½ cup diced pecans, and spoon a rounded teaspoon on top each mini cheesecake.

# Blueberries

## Blueberry Kuchen

Serves 6 to 8

Preheat oven to 350°F.

1 cup flour
1½ teaspoons baking powder
¾ teaspoon nutmeg
½ teaspoon salt
⅔ cup sugar
½ cup butter, room temperature
2 large eggs
1 teaspoon vanilla extract
2 teaspoons mandarin zest
1 cup blueberries, fresh or frozen
2 teaspoons cinnamon sugar (equal parts
   cinnamon and sugar)

I grew up in a German family accustomed to eating kuchen made the traditional way, with apples. We ate it for breakfast and at holidays. When friends gave me a copy of *A Taste of Wyoming* with the Blueberry Kuchen recipe, I had to try it. I can tell you it's yummy with blueberries, and equally tasty with sliced fresh baking apples.

In a large mixing bowl, combine flour, baking powder, nutmeg and salt. Set aside.
In another bowl, beat sugar and butter until creamy. Beat in eggs, vanilla, and mandarin zest; add to the flour mixture and combine.
Spread into an 8x8-inch buttered baking pan. Cover evenly with blueberries, and press berries lightly into batter. Sprinkle with cinnamon sugar. Bake 35 to 40 minutes, or until lightly browned. Cool slightly before serving.

# Lemon and Blueberry Tea Cake

Serves 8 to 10

Preheat oven to 375°F.

2 cups flour
2 teaspoons baking powder
¼ teaspoon salt
½ teaspoon cinnamon
1¼ cups sugar
¼ cup butter, room temperature
1 egg
½ cup half and half
½ cup sour cream
2 Meyer lemons, juiced
2½ cups fresh blueberries
2 tablespoons lemon zest

Sift flour, baking powder, salt and cinnamon together. Set aside.
Cream sugar and butter together using an electric mixer. Add egg, half and half, sour cream, and lemon juice. Blend until smooth. With mixer on low speed, slowly add flour until thoroughly mixed.

Fold in blueberries and lemon zest.
Pour batter into a greased 9x5-inch loaf pan.
Sprinkle streusel topping over batter.
Bake 50 minutes, or until top is golden brown and a toothpick inserted comes out clean.
Remove from oven and cool 5 minutes. Remove cake from pan and cool on a wire rack.

## Streusel Topping
¼ cup sugar
¼ cup brown sugar
⅓ cup flour
¼ cup butter, room temperature
½ teaspoon cinnamon

To make topping, combine all ingredients in a small mixing bowl with a pastry cutter or fork, almost to cornmeal texture.

Fresh blueberries are best in this recipe; frozen berries make a denser cake, but still delicious.

# May 28
# Cherries

Walnut Crostini with Ricotta Cheese and Cherries
Baked Cherries with Taleggio Cheese
Cherry and Apricot Topping
Pork Chops with Cherry Balsamic Sauce
Cherry Pie

My memory of eating cherries goes back to the first time our family took a driving tour from Minnesota to California. We drove thorough Utah and stopped at a small motel for a night's rest. For dessert we had cherry pie. I'll never forget the sensation on my taste buds with my first taste of sour cherry pie—taste buds never forget.

Years passed before I found my first crop of sour cherries. Now that I have a readily available source, cherry pies are a favorite at our house. June is cherry pie season (just in time for Father's Day) and during June we have more than our fair share of cherry pies. Cherries freeze well, and the freezer always has several bags of pitted sweet and sour cherries to enjoy during the year.

# Cherries

## Walnut Crostini with Ricotta Cheese and Cherries

Serves 4

Preheat oven to 375°F.

½ loaf walnut bread
1 tablespoon olive oil
Salt and pepper to taste
4 ounces ricotta cheese
1 pint cherries, pitted and quartered
2 tablespoons honey

To make crostini, slice bread in half length-wise, then cut in ¼-inch thick slices and place on a sheet tray.

Drizzle with olive oil and season lightly with salt and pepper. Toast in oven until crisp, 7 to 10 minutes.

Season ricotta lightly with salt and pepper. Spread generously on crostini.

Top each piece with a few cherry quarters and drizzle with honey.

Most artisan bakeries feature a nut bread, most often walnut. It gives any crostini recipe a little extra taste and texture.

# Baked Cherries with Taleggio Cheese

Serves 4

Preheat oven to broil.

2 cups cherries, pitted
4 ounces Taleggio cheese
1 loaf artisan bread, sliced ½-inch thick

Divide cherries into 4 six-ounce ramekins and top with cheese. Broil 5 to 7 minutes, until cheese is browned and bubbly.
Serve with grilled or toasted artisan bread.

# Cherry and Apricot Topping

Makes 2 cups

1 cup cherries, pitted and halved
2 apricots, pitted and sliced
1 cup strawberries, sliced
2 tablespoons orange juice
2 teaspoons sugar

Combine all ingredients.

> Simple combinations of seasonal fruit are a perfect addition to a bowl of vanilla ice cream or slice of angel food cake. We include a little sugar to sweeten and release the natural juices in the fruit, and citrus juice to add another level of acidity.

*Real dirt. Real food. Real health.*

# Cherries

## Pork Chops with Cherry Balsamic Sauce

Serves 4

Preheat grill.

¼ cup butter

½ onion, diced

2 cloves garlic, minced

¼ cup balsamic vinegar

3 cups cherries, halved

¼ cup chicken stock

Salt and pepper to taste

4 bone-in pork chops

1 tablespoon olive oil

In a medium saucepan, heat 2 tablespoons butter and cook onions and garlic until fragrant. Stir in vinegar and simmer 1 minute. Add cherries and stock and cook over medium high heat to reduce by one half. Remove from heat and whisk in remaining butter. Season to taste with salt and pepper. Transfer to a separate bowl.

Season pork chops with oil, salt and pepper and grill on both sides. Brush with some of the cherry juice reduction after turning.

To serve, arrange pork chops on a large platter and top with cherries.

# Cherry Pie

Serves 8

Preheat oven to 400°F.

## Two crust pie dough for 9-inch pie

¼ cup vegetable shortening

¼ cup butter

1½ cups all purpose flour

½ teaspoon salt

¼ cup cold water

½ teaspoon cinnamon

½ teaspoon sugar (mix with cinnamon)

½ teaspoon Demerara sugar (optional)

Use a pie dough cutter to blend shortening, butter, flour and salt to cornmeal stage. Slowly add cold water, mixing with a fork, until dough comes together. Add more water if necessary. Form into a ball, cover and chill at least 2 hours before rolling out.

Cut dough ball into 2 pieces, one slightly larger than the other. Roll out the dough on a floured surface until ⅛-inch thick. Make dough 10 inches for bottom, and 9 inches for top.

Place filling in shell. Apply top crust. Trim, roll and crimp edges. Score the dough 6 or 7 places to allow air to vent. Sprinkle top with cinnamon sugar mixture, then Demerara.

## Filling

5 cups sour or semi-sour cherries, pitted

1 cup sugar

¼ cup orange or tangelo juice

⅓ cup tapioca flour

½ teaspoon salt

2 teaspoons orange zest

½ teaspoon almond extract

1 tablespoon butter

Blend together cherries, sugar, juice, tapioca flour, salt, orange zest, almond extract. Stir gently and let stand 20 minutes.

Stir again, and spoon mixture into pie shell and distribute small pieces of butter over the fruit. Cover with remaining piece of dough.

Bake pie until a toothpick inserted comes out clean and juices are bubbling around the crust, 50 to 60 minutes.

ℰ⌒ The secret to flaky pie crust is chilling the crust before rolling it out. Form the dough into a ball, cover it, and put it in the refrigerator for 2 to 6 hours. Take the ball out of the refrigerator and let it sit just long enough to take the chill off before rolling it out.

*From the top:*
*Chestnut*
*Provence*
*Heirloom Cannellini*
*Black Turtle*
*White Emergo*
*Grand Mother Stallard*

# Dried Beans

Lamb and White Bean Soup

Black Bean and Spicy Sausage Stew

Apple Juice Baked Beans

Baked Beans

Loaded with nutrients and full of fiber, beans are available bagged or bulk at grocery and natural food stores. Several kinds of beans live in our cupboard, allowing us to cook beans for a soup or side dish almost at a moment's notice.

Several local growers package their heirloom beans and we like to try something other than pinto or black beans, the staples of Latin American and Caribbean cuisine. We use Navy beans and Boston beans for baked beans or soups. Another good bet is the cannellini bean, which is more delicate in flavor. The heirloom cannellini is a real taste treat. When serving beans with lamb, our favorite is the flageolet (pronounced flah-joh-lay), the small creamy beans used by the French.

Cooking times for beans differs depending on the age of the bean. Older beans take forever to soften. Purchase beans in small amounts so you have fresher tasting, faster cooking beans. And remember, canned beans are less flavorful and saltier than reconstituted dried beans.

Don't hesitate to substitute one kind of bean for another. There are hundreds, perhaps thousands of beans on the market.

*Have a glass of wine with dinner.*
*—Michael Pollan*

# Dried Beans

## Lamb and White Bean Soup

Serves 8

2 tablespoons olive oil

2 to 3 pounds lamb neck pieces

2 cups onions, diced

1 cup carrots, sliced

3 celery stalks, sliced

2 large garlic cloves, minced

4 cups chicken broth

2 bay leaves

2 teaspoons salt

½ teaspoon pepper

1 teaspoon each thyme and marjoram leaves

3 cups cooked or canned small white
   beans, drained

Heat olive oil in a 5-quart Dutch oven. Add lamb pieces and brown over medium heat. Remove from pan. Add onions, carrots, celery and garlic to pan. Cook until soft. Return lamb to pan, add broth, seasonings and herbs. Simmer 2 hours. Cool, and remove meat and bay leaves from soup. Pull meat away from bones, cut into bite size pieces and return to pot. Chill and skim fat. Stir in beans. Heat and serve.

For a thicker soup, add ½ to 1 cup mashed potatoes or 1 cup of thinly sliced white or whole wheat bread (crusts removed) and stir.

*Soup is a lot like family. Each ingredient enhances the others; each batch has its own characteristics; and it needs time to simmer to reach full flavor.* —Marge Kennedy

## Black Bean and Spicy Sausage Stew

Serves 6

*Thanks to Dan Macon of Flying Mule Farm for this recipe.*

2 teaspoons grapeseed oil

1 pound Argentine sausage

3 cloves garlic, minced

¼ teaspoon allspice

2½ cups black beans, cooked

1½ cups tomatoes, diced

2 Anaheim peppers, roasted and diced

Salt and pepper to taste

2 cups brown rice, cooked

In a large sauté pan, heat oil and sauté sausage until lightly browned. Add garlic and allspice and sauté 1 minute. Stir in beans, tomatoes and peppers and simmer 4 to 5 minutes. Season to taste with salt and pepper. Serve over brown rice.

# Apple Juice Baked Beans

Serves 6 to 8

Preheat oven to 300°F.

1 pound dried pinto beans
3 cups fresh apple juice
½ cup apple cider vinegar
8 ounces salt pork or cured ham, thinly sliced
2 small yellow onions, diced
½ cup sorghum molasses
1 tablespoon brown mustard
2 teaspoons salt

Cover beans with water and soak overnight. Drain beans and place in a heavy 3-quart sauce pan. Add apple juice and vinegar and bring to a boil. Simmer gently over low heat 30 minutes. Remove from heat, drain beans and save liquid.

Place half of salt pork or ham on the bottom of a 2-quart Pyrex baking dish. Layer with beans and onions; repeat until all beans and onions are used. Top with beans. Place remaining pork on top of beans.

In a small bowl whisk molasses, mustard and salt until blended. Pour evenly over beans.

Cover dish, and bake 4 hours.

Stir beans. Add additional saved apple juice if beans are dry. Replace cover and bake until beans are tender, up to 2 hours.

# Baked Beans

Serves 6 to 8

Preheat oven to 300°F.

1 pound cranberry beans
½ cup dark molasses
½ cup dark brown sugar
1 heaping tablespoon dry mustard
4 bay leaves
1 heaping tablespoon salt
½ teaspoon pepper
1 can diced tomatoes (14.5 ounces)
6 cups bean water from soaking beans
10 to 12 ounces ham or salt pork,
   sliced into 4 equal pieces
1 pound torpedo onions, diced
20 cloves, wrapped in 6x6-inch cheese cloth
Salt and pepper to taste

Soak beans overnight in cold water. Use at least 6 cups water. Drain beans and save bean water. Set aside.

In a saucepan, combine molasses, brown sugar, mustard, bay leaves, salt, pepper, tomatoes, bean water and cook until hot. Set aside.

Place sliced ham or salt pork on the bottom of an 8x11-inch roasting pan. Sprinkle diced onions over meat. Add cloves. Place drained beans over onions.

Pour hot molasses mixture over beans and cover pan (aluminum foil will do).

Bake 6 hours (new crop beans need less baking time). Check beans every hour; add more hot bean water if necessary. Test for doneness after 3 hours. Remove cover for last hour of baking. Remove from oven. Discard cloves. Shred meat and return to pan. Add salt and pepper if desired.

*June 11*

# Arugula

Grilled Pizza

Pasta with Arugula and Chili Flakes

Blue Cheese Burgers

Arugula Crusted Leg of Lamb with Oranges and Flageolet Beans

*I*magine a kitchen full of women, all of them intent on a task, and all wearing a handmade apron. My head is full of memories of women in aprons cooking – at church suppers, big family camping trips, and, perhaps best, of my aunts baking in the family kitchen.

Good things happen around real food, and sisters preparing meals together for a family gathering makes a lovely memory. Everything was made from scratch. The flavors were rich and complex and honest. And those aprons! I can picture a woman at the fabric store selecting just the right piece of cloth. The apron would be washed often, so the fabric had to be sturdy and durable, yet an appropriate design – fruits or vegetables or flowers, something that said food was made from real food grown from the ground.

Wearing aprons is popular again. Perhaps it's because people are beginning to realize food made in our own kitchen definitely tastes better. And why wouldn't we want to be feeding our families healthy tasty food and making memories?

# Arugula

## Grilled Pizza

Makes 4 medium pizzas

*Thanks to Debbie Dutra for this recipe.*

Heat grill before assembling pizza.

### Whole-wheat Pizza Dough

1 envelope dry active yeast
2 cups warm water
2½ cups all purpose flour, plus more for dusting
2 teaspoons salt
2 cups whole wheat flour
Oil for dough bowl

Dissolve yeast in warm water in a large bowl and let stand 5 minutes. Stir in 2 cups all purpose flour and salt. Stir in whole wheat flour. Add remaining all purpose flour, 1 tablespoon at a time, until dough comes away from the bowl but is still a little sticky.

Knead dough on a lightly floured board about 5 minutes, until dough springs back when poked. Place in a lightly oiled bowl, turn to coat all sides of dough. Let dough rise about 4 hours. Divide in 4 portions, roll in balls. (You may freeze the extra dough balls.) Wrap each portion in parchment paper with a little dusting of flour.

### Fresh Tomato Pizza Sauce

Makes about 4 cups

¼ cup olive oil
2 cloves shallots, diced
3 to 4 cloves garlic, minced
1½ baskets cherry tomatoes
2 cups fresh basil leaves
Salt to taste

Heat oil in large pan, and sauté shallots and garlic. Add tomatoes, basil and salt to taste. Cook on low heat 1 hour. Let cool, then purée cooled mixture. Can be used right away or frozen for later.

## Herb Garden Pesto Pizza Sauce

Makes about ½ cup

1 clove garlic
¼ cup fresh mint leaves
¼ cup basil leaves
¼ cup chives
6 tablespoons olive oil
Salt to taste

Purée all ingredients except salt until smooth and well mixed. Add salt to taste. Use liberally on pizza or in salad dressing.

To assemble and bake pizzas: Roll each dough ball out to ⅓-inch thick. Brush barbecue grill with olive oil. Place dough on hot grill. Within minutes air bubbles will appear inside and large bubbled areas will appear on outside of dough. Turn dough over and cook other side. Turn barbecue grill to low, and start building pizza. Add sauce first, then cheese and toppings. Close lid and cook on low, or with barbecue off, 5 minutes. If using meat, cook prior to adding it to pizza.

> ⤳ We used this recipe when friends gathered for camp-outs on Donner Lake near Truckee, California. One person was in charge of pizza dough. Everyone who came brought toppings, and we created all sorts of pizzas cooked over an open fire grill.
>
> Each pizza started with sauce, then Parmesan or mozzarella cheese (or both). Pizza topping ingredients include: arugula and fennel, sautéed onions and cooked sausage, tomato and purple basil leaves, and more. The pizzas were delicious and loaded with flavor. Use your imagination to create your own masterpieces.

# Pasta with Arugula and Chili Flakes

Serves 4

1 pound whole wheat penne pasta
½ cup olive oil
6 cloves garlic, whole
2 leeks, sliced
1 to 2 teaspoons chili flakes
Salt and pepper to taste
3 cups arugula, large leaves torn in pieces
¼ cup Parmesan cheese, grated

Cook pasta in boiling salted water until tender. Drain and set aside.
In a small saucepan, heat oil and add garlic cloves. Simmer gently 10 minutes, careful not to let garlic brown. Remove from heat and let stand 15 minutes. Smash cloves and set aside; reserve garlic oil.
In a large sauté pan, heat 2 tablespoons garlic oil and sauté leeks until softened, about 3 minutes. Add chili flakes, smashed garlic, and season with salt and pepper and then add arugula and cooked pasta. Heat to wilt arugula. Top with Parmesan cheese and serve.

*www.theartofrealfood.com*

# Arugula

## Blue Cheese Burgers

Serves 4

Preheat grill.

1½ pounds ground beef
1 teaspoon Worcestershire sauce
Salt and pepper to taste
¼ cup blue cheese
4 ciabatta rolls
¼ cup mayonnaise
1 cup arugula leaves
2 tomatoes, sliced
1 red onion, sliced

In a medium bowl, combine beef and Worcestershire. Season liberally with salt and pepper, and form into 4 balls. Place 1 tablespoon blue cheese in the center of each, and carefully flatten out to a patty shape.

Grill burgers until medium rare. Place buns on grill to toast. To assemble, spread mayonnaise on buns, then layer with arugula, patties, tomatoes and onion.

> ℰ Our neighborhood butcher always buys meat at the local county fair junior livestock auction – meat raised by 4-H and Future Farmers of America members. It's important to know where our food comes from. I know the lamb, beef and pork available at the local butcher shop is healthy for all the right reasons: the meat is raised locally; by purchasing this meat we're enforcing the value of healthy meat and farming; and we're supporting our neighborhood butcher.

# Arugula Crusted Leg of Lamb with Oranges and Flageolet Beans

Serves 8

Preheat oven to 400°F.

1 tablespoon plus ½ cup olive oil
½ onion, diced
1 carrot, peeled and cut into quarters
2 stalks celery, halved
1 pound flageolet beans
Salt and pepper to taste
2 cloves garlic, chopped
1 lemon, juiced
2 cups arugula leaves
2½ pounds boneless leg of lamb
3 oranges, segmented

In a large pot, heat 1 tablespoon olive oil and cook onions until fragrant. Add carrot, celery, beans and enough water to cover. Bring to a boil and reduce heat to simmer about 1 hour, until beans are tender. Season to taste with salt and pepper. Remove and discard carrots and celery stalks. Drain remaining liquid. Set beans aside.

In a food processor, purée garlic, lemon juice, arugula and ½ cup olive oil. Season with salt and pepper. Set aside.

Tie lamb with butchers twine if necessary and coat with arugula mixture. Roast 15 minutes, then reduce heat to 325°F and continue cooking until desired doneness.

To serve, place beans on a large platter, and top with sliced lamb and orange segments.

*June 18*

# Summer Squash

Roasted Summer Squash with Roasted Cherry Tomatoes
Sautéed Summer Squash with Almonds
Quinoa and Summer Squash Stuffed Tomatoes
Summer Squash Gratin

Seed catalogs that date back to 1828 listed summer squash. It has been a staple crop in the Americas for millennia. Native Americans grew yellow crookneck. In fact, the word "squash" is thought to be derived from a Native American word meaning "food eaten raw." Summer squash comes in an assortment of shapes and colors: dark green, sunny yellow, striped, elongated, short and stubby, even scalloped.

One of my favorite ways to prepare slightly oversized summer squash is to slice it, dip it in egg, then matzoh meal, then lightly sauté each side until golden brown. Sometimes, that's dinner.

Summer squash is without a doubt the most dependable vegetable in the summer garden. Plant it and you're likely to have enough to eat practically every day and still have enough to share with the neighbors. But just because summer squash is plentiful doesn't mean it can't be part of an uncommon meal.

# Summer Squash

## Roasted Summer Squash with Roasted Cherry Tomatoes

Serves 4

Preheat oven to 400°F.

3 cups summer squash, large diced
1 tablespoon plus 1 teaspoon olive oil
Salt and pepper to taste
1 pint cherry tomatoes
3 tablespoons Parmesan cheese, grated

Season squash with 1 tablespoon oil, salt and pepper and roast on a sheet tray 10 to 15 minutes, until fork tender. Repeat process with tomatoes, using 1 teaspoon olive oil, and roast until just blistered, 8 to 10 minutes. Toss together with cheese.

## Sautéed Summer Squash with Almonds

Serves 4

2 tablespoons grapeseed oil
3 cups summer squash, large diced
1 clove garlic, minced
1 large shallot, sliced
¼ cup sliced almonds, toasted
Salt and pepper to taste

Heat oil in a large sauté pan and add squash. Sauté until beginning to caramelize. Add garlic and shallot and continue to cook 1 to 2 minutes. Stir in almonds and season to taste with salt and pepper.

## Quinoa and Summer Squash Stuffed Tomatoes

Serves 6

1½ cups red quinoa
2 tablespoons grapeseed oil
2 cups summer squash, diced
¼ cup red onions, diced
2 cloves garlic, minced
¼ cup basil, chiffonade
2 tablespoons red wine vinegar
Salt and pepper to taste
6 large heirloom tomatoes
6 basil leaves

Bring 3½ cups salted water and quinoa to a boil. Reduce heat to simmer, cover and cook 20 to 25 minutes, until grain is tender. Drain excess water; place quinoa in a large bowl and set aside. Heat oil in a large sauté pan, and cook squash until it begins to caramelize. Add onions and garlic, and cook until fragrant. Add squash mixture to quinoa and season to taste with basil, vinegar, salt and pepper.
Cut top quarter off tomatoes and, using a melon baller or small spoon, carefully remove seeds and juices. Season tomatoes with salt and pepper and fill with quinoa mixture. Garnish with basil leaves.

## Summer Squash Gratin

Preheat oven to 400°F.

Serves 4

1 small eggplant, sliced ¼-inch thick
2 small zucchini or yellow squashes, sliced ¼-inch thick
1 teaspoon salt
¼ cup olive oil
4 cloves garlic, minced
Salt and pepper to taste
1 loaf artisan bread, (crusts removed), sliced ½-inch thick
¼ cup basil, chiffonade
¼ cup Parmesan cheese, grated

In a colander, toss eggplant and zucchini with salt and let stand 20 minutes; drain well. Set aside. In a small bowl, combine oil and garlic. Season lightly with salt and pepper.
Coat bottom of 8-inch round baking dish with 2 teaspoons garlic oil. Tear bread into 2-inch pieces and thoroughly cover bottom of dish. Drizzle half the garlic oil and 2 tablespoons basil over bread. Arrange eggplant and zucchini in dish, overlapping as necessary. Season lightly with salt and pepper. Top with remaining oil, basil and Parmesan.
Bake 25 to 35 minutes, until bottom of bread is golden brown and cheese is melted. Remove from oven and let stand 10 minutes before serving.

*June 25*

# Nectarines

Nectarines with Honey and Almonds
Nectarine Galette
Nectarine and Blueberry Pie
Nectarine and Blackberry Pie
Dessert Crepes with Nectarines and Blackberries

Nectarines are believed to have originated as a mutant peach with a smooth instead of a fuzzy skin. They have a perkier flavor than their peach cousins, as though they are telling the world they are their own distinctive fruit.

Use nectarines the same way you'd use peaches: add to a green salad with spring onions, make chutney as an accompaniment to grilled meat, or simply slice, add a drizzle of honey and serve as dessert.

Nectarines are great baked, or sliced over buttermilk pancakes or homemade waffles with maple syrup. During nectarine season, we like puréeing the fruit to use in fruit cocktails or to add sweetness to a bowl of cherries. Puréed nectarines freeze well and keep for three or four months.

## Nectarines with Honey and Almonds

Serves 4

4 nectarines, pitted and cut into wedges
1 cup Greek yogurt
2 tablespoons honey
¼ cup sliced almonds, toasted

Arrange nectarines in 4 small serving bowls. Top with yogurt and honey, and garnish with almonds...a simple but delicious summer dessert! Serve with a glass of champagne.

# Nectarines

## Nectarine Galette

Serves 6

Preheat oven to 400°F.

### Galette dough for 9-inch pie pan

3 tablespoons vegetable shortening
3 tablespoons cold butter
1 cup all purpose flour
¼ teaspoon salt
3 tablespoons cold water
½ teaspoon cinnamon
½ teaspoon sugar (mix with cinnamon)
½ teaspoon Demerara sugar (optional)

Use a pie dough cutter to blend shortening, butter, flour and salt to cornmeal stage. Slowly add cold water, mixing with a fork, until dough comes together. Add more water if necessary. Form into a ball, cover and chill at least 2 hours before rolling out.

In the palm of your hand, form ball into round flat disk. Roll dough on a floured surface until it is ⅛-inch thick. Dough will be 14 to16 inches in diameter. Place in bottom of 9-inch pie pan; dough will fall off edges of pan. Set aside.

### Filling

½ cup sugar
3 tablespoons tapioca flour
½ teaspoon salt
½ teaspoon almond extract
4½ cups nectarines, skin on, sliced
2 teaspoons cold butter

In a large bowl, blend sugar, tapioca flour, salt, and almond extract and nectarines. Stir gently and let stand 20 minutes.

Stir again, and spoon mixture into center of galette shell and distribute small pieces of butter over the fruit.

Bring edges of dough toward the center over the fruit and staple to the fruit with toothpicks. There will be a small opening in the middle. Sprinkle top of crust with cinnamon sugar, then Demerara. Bake until a toothpick inserted comes out clean and juices are bubbling around the crust, 45 to 50 minutes.

# Nectarine and Blueberry Pie

Serves 8

Preheat oven to 400°F.

## Two crust pie dough for 9-inch pie

¼ cup vegetable shortening
¼ cup cold butter
1½ cups all purpose flour
½ teaspoon salt
¼ cup cold water
½ teaspoon cinnamon
½ teaspoon sugar (mix with cinnamon)
1 teaspoon Demerara sugar (optional)

Use a pie dough cutter to blend shortening, butter, flour and salt to cornmeal stage. Slowly add cold water, mixing with a fork, until dough comes together. Add more water if necessary. Form into a ball, cover and chill at least 2 hours before rolling out.
Cut dough ball into two pieces, one slightly larger than the other. Roll out dough on a floured surface until ⅛-inch thick. Make dough 10 inches for bottom, and 9 inches for top.

Place filling in shell. Apply top crust. Trim, roll and crimp edges. Score the dough 6 or 7 places to allow air to vent. Sprinkle top with cinnamon sugar mixture, then Demerara.

## Filling

3 cups nectarines, sliced
1½ cups whole blueberries
⅔ cup sugar
⅓ cup tapioca flour
½ teaspoon salt
½ teaspoon almond extract
1 tablespoon cold butter

In a large bowl place nectarines, blueberries, sugar, tapioca flour, salt and almond extract. Stir gently and let stand 20 minutes.
Stir again, and spoon mixture into pie shell and distribute small pieces of butter over the fruit. Bake pie until juices are bubbling on the edge of the crust, about 50 minutes.

# Nectarines

## Nectarine and Blackberry Pie

Serves 8

Preheat oven to 400°F.

### Two crust pie dough for 9-inch pie

¼ cup vegetable shortening

¼ cup cold butter

1½ cups all purpose flour

½ teaspoon salt

¼ cup cold water

½ teaspoon cinnamon

½ teaspoon sugar (mix with cinnamon)

1 teaspoon Demerara sugar (optional)

Use a pie dough cutter to blend shortening, butter, flour and salt to cornmeal stage. Slowly add cold water, mixing with a fork, until dough comes together. Add more water if necessary. Form into a ball, cover and chill at least 2 hours before rolling out.

Cut dough ball into two pieces, one slightly larger than the other. Roll out dough on a floured surface until ⅛-inch thick. Make dough 10 inches for bottom, and 9 inches for top.

Place filling in shell. Apply top crust. Trim, roll and crimp edges. Score the dough 6 or 7 places to allow air to vent. Sprinkle top with cinnamon sugar mixture, then Demerara.

### Filling

3 cups nectarines, unpeeled, sliced

2 cups wild or domestic blackberries

1 cup sugar

1 teaspoon orange zest

1 teaspoon almond extract

½ teaspoon salt

⅓ cup tapioca

1 tablespoon cold butter

In a large bowl place nectarines, blackberries, sugar, zest, almond extract, salt and tapioca. Stir gently and let stand 20 minutes.

Stir again, and spoon mixture into pie shell and distribute small pieces of butter over the fruit. Bake 50 to 60 minutes. Cool before slicing and serving.

Use the same recipe for other nectarine pies, replacing blackberries with boysenberries, marionberries, or olallieberries.

# Dessert Crepes with Nectarines and Blackberries

Serves 4

2 eggs, lightly beaten
⅔ cup whole milk
1 tablespoon butter, melted
½ cup all purpose flour
1 tablespoon white sugar
Dash salt
1 tablespoon grapeseed oil

Whisk eggs, milk, butter, flour, sugar and salt until blended.
Place crepe pan over medium heat. Add fine covering of oil. Spoon a scant ¼ cup of crepe batter into pan; tilt the pan to totally cover bottom with batter. Cook on medium heat until golden. Turn crepe over and cook another 30 to 45 seconds. Serve crepes warm with nectarine and blackberry filling. Garnish with whipped cream and powdered sugar.

## Nectarine and Blackberry Filling

2 cups nectarines, sliced
2 cups blackberries
⅓ cup sugar
1 tablespoon lemon juice

Place all ingredients in a bowl and marinate 15 to 20 minutes.

*July 2*

# Figs

Candied Dried Figs

Flatbread with Figs and Blue Cheese Cream

Fig Salad with Ginger Honey Vinaigrette

Angel Food Cake: 4th of July Cake & Rocky Road Cake

## Candied Dried Figs

*Thanks to Marianne Bierwagen for this recipe.*

2 cups sugar
½ cup water
5 pounds fresh figs

Place sugar and water in a large sauce pan. Bring to a boil. Add figs. Reduce heat to medium, cover pan and cook 1 hour. Set aside.

The next day bring figs to a medium boil, and slowly cook uncovered 1 hour. Set aside.

On day three, bring figs to a slow boil.

Immediately reduce heat and slowly simmer uncovered 1 hour, or until pan is just dry. Watch pan closely.

Cool figs in pan. Place on paper towels to dry. Let dry at least 2 hours.

Line sheet tray or cookie sheet with parchment paper, and place figs on parchment paper. Place in a sunny spot in the house to finish drying. Turn every day for a week, until no longer sticky. Replace parchment paper as needed.

Shape figs into the shape of a quarter. Dust with sugar if desired.

The figs freeze well.

Every year Chris Bierwagen of Bierwagen's Orchard in Chicago Park prepares his mother's recipe for candied figs. What a treat to receive these special figs as a holiday gift! The figs are delicate, moist, and delicious. Yes, the recipe takes three days to make, but it's worth it!

# Figs

## Flatbread with Figs and Blue Cheese Cream

Serves 4

Preheat oven to 400°F.

### Flatbread

2½ cups all purpose flour
2¾ teaspoons baking powder
1 teaspoon salt
¾ to 1 cup water
2 tablespoons olive oil
Salt and pepper to taste

In a food processor pulse flour, baking powder salt. Slowly add water and 1 tablespoon oil, and pulse until just combined. Remove dough, and knead on a floured surface to form a ball. Cover and refrigerate at least 1 hour.

Cut dough into 4 pieces and roll out on a floured surface to ⅛-inch thick. Place on sheet tray, coat lightly with remaining olive oil, salt and pepper to taste. Puncture with a fork to prevent air bubbles. Bake 20 to 25 minutes, until dough begins to brown and crisp. Remove and cool on a wire rack.

### Flatbread Topping

1 cup cream
1 to 2 ounces blue cheese
Salt and pepper to taste
2 baskets figs, sliced
½ cup bacon, diced and cooked
2 cups arugula

In a small saucepan, heat cream and reduce by half. Turn heat to low and stir in cheese. Season to taste with salt and pepper, and set aside.

To assemble, spread a thin layer of blue cheese cream on each piece of flatbread. Top with figs and bacon and bake 10 to 15 minutes. Remove from oven and top with arugula.

# Fig Salad with Ginger Honey Vinaigrette

Serves 4

1 head red leaf lettuce, torn into pieces
1 basket figs, sliced
1 ounce goat cheese, crumbled
¼ cup walnuts, toasted

## Ginger Honey Vinaigrette

¼ cup Champagne vinegar
1 teaspoon ginger, grated
1 teaspoon honey
½ cup olive oil
Salt and pepper to taste

Combine salad ingredients. Set aside.
Combine vinaigrette ingredients. Toss with salad ingredients and serve immediately.

# Angel Food Cake: 4th of July Cake and Rocky Road Cake

Serves 10 to 12

Preheat oven to 350°F.

1 cup cake flour
1½ cups sugar
½ teaspoon salt
1½ cups free-range egg whites (about 12 large eggs), room temperature
1 teaspoon cream of tartar
1 tablespoon Meyer lemon juice
1½ teaspoons vanilla extract

Sift flour, then measure, and place in a bowl. Add ½ cup sugar and salt to flour and sift twice more. Set aside.

Beat egg whites in a large, clean bowl. When whites are foamy, add cream of tartar, lemon juice and vanilla. When bubbles are uniform, add remaining cup of sugar a few tablespoons at a time. Beat whites until they form stiff peaks (when you lift the beaters a peak will form and hold) and sugar is dissolved.

Fold in the flour with a clean rubber spatula, using a down-the-side-and-up-through-the-batter motion. Do not over mix.

When mixture is thoroughly combined, turn into a very clean grease-free 10-inch tube pan.

Bake 50 minutes. Test for doneness by pressing lightly in center of cake; if it springs back, cake is done. Remove from oven and invert pan until cake is cool.

The cake must be raised an inch or more above the counter during cooling process. An easy way to do this is to invert the cake pan over a wine-type bottle. (see photo, page 24)

When cool, remove the cake by running a serrated knife around the edges of the pan.

Slice cake in half horizontally; there's enough angel food cake to make the 4th of July cake and the rocky road cake. You can freeze the half you don't use.

Angel food cake is a big hit with everyone. It's made with egg whites and not too much sugar, and it provides a nice light finish to a simple meal.

# 4th of July Cake with Meyer Lemon Cream Cheese Icing

½ angel food cake sliced horizontally
    (recipe on previous page)
Meyer lemon cream cheese icing (recipe below)
1 cup fresh blueberries
1 cup fresh raspberries or strawberries

Gently pour Meyer lemon cream cheese icing over cake, letting it dribble down the sides (photo, previous page). Use blueberries and raspberries (or strawberries) to alternate colors on the top of the icing. Bingo! Red, white and blue!

## Meyer Lemon Cream Cheese Icing

3 ounces Gina Marie cream cheese, room
    temperature
1½ tablespoons half and half or heavy cream
¾ cup confectioners sugar, sifted
1 tablespoon Meyer lemon zest

Whip cream cheese and cream until fluffy. Slowly add sifted sugar. Add lemon zest and blend. For an orange flavored icing, replace the lemon zest with orange zest.

# Rocky Road Cake

6 ounces chocolate chips
2 egg whites
2 cups organic heavy cream
2 teaspoons sugar
1 teaspoon vanilla
½ angel food cake (recipe on previous page)
1 cup pecans or walnuts, chopped

Melt chocolate in a double boiler, set aside to cool.
Beat egg whites until stiff, and fold in melted chocolate.
In a large bowl, whip cream, add sugar and vanilla; fold egg white/chocolate mixture into whipped cream. Set aside.
Tear angel food cake into bite-size pieces.
In a 9x13-inch buttered baking dish, alternate a layer of cake with a layer of cream mixture. Top with nuts.
Refrigerate 6 to 12 hours before serving.

We prefer Sweet Earth Chocolate semisweet baking chips (42%) or melting chips (54%); a good substitute is Ghirardelli cocoa chips (60%).

# Cucumbers

Ahi Poke Cucumber Boats

Smoked Salmon Spread with Sliced Cucumbers

Ice Cold Shrimp Soup

Kosher Dill Pickles (refrigerated)

*F*ermented foods are thought to be one of the oldest forms of preserves. Found in cuisines around the globe, fermented foods include cheese, yogurt, salami, surstömming (pickled herring), miso, sauerkraut, salsa and chutney. As the raw ingredients ferment, their flavor becomes more exciting. Their nutritional value becomes more exciting, too. Often called "super foods," fermented foods have probiotics that aid digestion, promote the absorption of nutrients and strengthen the immune system, including its ability to fight allergies. They are also rich in enzymes, B vitamins and Omega-3 fatty acids.

# Cucumbers

## Ahi Poke Cucumber Boats

Serves 8

### Ahi Poke

Makes 2 cups

1 pound fresh sushi grade ahi, small diced
3 to 4 tablespoons soy sauce
1 teaspoon sesame oil
½ to 1 teaspoon chili oil
1 teaspoon each black and white sesame seeds
½ cup scallions, sliced
Salt and pepper to taste

Combine all ingredients and season to taste with salt and pepper. Keep chilled.

### Cucumber Boats

8 small Persian cucumbers, halved lengthwise
2 cups ahi poke
2 teaspoons sesame seeds
½ cup scallions, sliced

Remove seeds from cucumber halves, careful not to puncture skin. Top with ahi poke and garnish with sesame seeds and scallions.

# Smoked Salmon Spread with Sliced Cucumbers

Serves 8

1 cup smoked salmon spread (purchased)
½ cup crème fraîche
1 artisan baguette, sliced ½-inch thick
1 large English cucumber, sliced ⅛-inch thick

Combine smoked salmon spread with crème fraîche; spread on each piece of bread. Garnish with fanned cucumber slices for an easy and elegant appetizer.

We're fortunate to have a wonderful fish company at our local farmers market that sells smoked salmon spread as well as seasoned ahi poke. Although it's fun to make from scratch, sometimes it's more convenient to purchase the finished product.

# Ice Cold Shrimp Soup

Serves 4

1 pound large shrimp

1 cup fresh corn

1 cup Persian or English cucumbers, sliced
  into ½-inch pieces

¼ cup basil, diced

½ cup torpedo onions, sliced into ½-inch pieces

¼ cup red and yellow bell peppers, sliced
  into ½-inch pieces

3 cups tomatoes, grated into pulp

3 tablespoons olive oil

½ cup red wine vinegar

1 teaspoon salt

½ teaspoon pepper

1 ripe avocado (optional)

Basil leaves for garnish

Remove shells from shrimp, devein, and cook in boiling water 2 minutes. Drain, rinse in cold water, and refrigerate.

To make soup place remaining ingredients, except avocado and basil leaves, in a large bowl. Cover and refrigerate.

To serve, place cold soup in bowls. Slice each shrimp in half lengthwise, and place 5 pieces of halved shrimp on top of soup, add two or three slices of avocado, and garnish with a basil leaf. Serve with sliced baguettes.

*No occupation is so delightful to me as the culture of the earth, and no culture comparable to that of the garden.*
*—Thomas Jefferson*

# Cucumbers

## Kosher Dill Pickles (refrigerated)

Makes 1 gallon

5 to 7 pounds small Persian cucumbers, rinsed
12 dill flower heads or 2 tablespoons dried dill
   weed and 2 tablespoons dill seed
15 cloves garlic
8 black peppercorns
½ teaspoon chili flakes
⅓ cup Kosher salt

Place cucumbers in 1-gallon jar. Fill to top.
Add dill, garlic, peppercorns and chili flakes.
Dissolve salt in 1 quart of water. Add salt water
to jar and finish filling with plain water.
Add a weight to keep cucumbers under water; do
not cover the jar.
Store in a cool, dry place, and ferment 10 to 11
days.

### Fermentation sequence:

1 to 3 days: Clear brine, no cloudiness
2 to 3 days: Cloudy brine with gas formation
5 to 6 days: Cloudy brine with no gas formation
Move pickles into quart jars, fill with brine, cover
with a lid and refrigerate.

> More than 25 years of experience
> tells me to use very small whole Persian-style
> cucumbers. More fit in a gallon jar, and
> smaller cucumbers stay crunchy longer.
>
> Always put the jar in a cool, dark place
> during the fermentation process. For us, the
> basement floor is the coolest spot.

Chili flakes are crushed hot dried red peppers. They're perfect for pickling, chowders, cioppino, spaghetti sauce, pizza sauce, soups, sausage and more. As chili flakes have become more popular, the varieties of crushed red peppers used have changed, though the mix typically includes ancho, bell, cayenne and others. Often there is a high ratio of seeds, which intensifies the heat of this flavorful condiment.

I recently learned a lesson about chili flakes the hard way. It was rainy and cold – just the right kind of evening for cioppino. As I sprinkled chili flakes into the broth, according to the recipe, of course, I forgot I was using a bottle of fresh chili flakes. The heat of the broth was intense; it cooled down after adding the seafood, but the cioppino didn't totally calm down until a day later.

My advice: add a small amount of chili flakes and take a taste. It's easy to add more heat, and almost impossible to remove it.

# It's All About Fat!

It's a common misconception that fats make you fat. While it is true that too much of anything will pack on the pounds, fats are a vital nutrient. If you've ever tried a low-fat diet, you probably felt hungry all the time as though you were deprived. The reason lies in the very thing a low-fat diet is lacking: adequate amounts of fat. Fats slow digestion, which keeps you feeling full and satisfied for longer periods of time. Fats also enhance the flavor of food.

Fats also supply essential fatty acids (EFAs) Omega-3 and 6, which the body needs to operate. EFAs are building blocks for every bodily process you can think of, including brain cell function, nervous system activity, hormone production and immune system operation. Like other nutrients, your body cannot manufacture EFAs, but takes what it needs from the foods you eat.

Particular attention is being paid to Omega-3 for two reasons. First, Omega-3 has amazing anti-inflammatory properties which have been linked to the prevention and treatment of health problems including heart disease, diabetes, arthritis, osteoporosis and skin disorders. Second, the typical diet is heavy in Omega-6 and light in, even devoid, of Omega-3.

Omega-3 is especially important for women. Scientists have linked menstrual symptoms such as cramping, headaches and nausea to low Omega-3 concentrations in the blood. Omega-3 also increases fertility, reduces the risk of premature birth, aids in fetal brain development and can curtail post-partum depression. For women entering menopause, Omega-3 reduces hot flashes, prevents and treats osteoporosis and acts as a mood stabilizer. For women of all ages, Omega-3 helps maintain radiant skin, lustrous hair, and strong nails. You can find Omega-3 in cold water fish (salmon, halibut and sardines). Other sources include walnuts, flaxseed, broccoli, cauliflower and dark green leafy vegetables.

Omega-6 is found in nuts, seeds, soy and the oils extracted from them. These oils—especially soy—are the ones most frequently used in making packaged snack foods, ready-meals and fast foods, all of which are frequent guests at American tables.

The problem is Omega-6 tends to promote inflammation (a necessary immune response). In a healthy diet, Omega-3 and Omega-6 work together keeping inflammation in check. But a diet heavy in processed foods allows inflammation and inflammation-related disease to run rampant.

Olive oil is not on the list of sources for Omega-3 or 6 because olive oil is an Omega-9 fat. Omega-9 is often grouped with EFAs but doesn't actually qualify as one because our bodies are able to manufacture small amounts of it. Nonetheless, Omega-9 is a "good" fat that lowers cholesterol, strengthens the immune system and provides protection against certain kinds of cancer. Other sources of Omega-9 include avocados, almonds, peanuts and sesame oil.

> For more information about Omega-3, visit eatwild.com and see what author Jo Robinson has to say about healthy, natural and nutritious grass-fed beef, lamb, poultry, pork, goat and other wild edibles.

# Tomatoes

Ground Cherry Salsa

Jerry's Tomato Salsa

Tomato Gratin

Pork Tenderloin with Ground Cherries

Beef Ribs with Classic Barbecue Sauce

Tomato Braised Short Ribs with Pasta

Plum and Ground Cherry Pie

No other vegetable evokes more passion than the tomato, especially heirloom tomatoes, those gems from the past bursting with flavor and character. Even their names sound romantic and exciting: Costoluto Genovese, Nebraska Wedding, Purple Calabash, and more. Not only do they add wonderful flavors to recipes, they add a bit of history.

# Tomatoes

## Ground Cherry Salsa

Serves 4

½ cup ground cherries, husked and halved
½ cup English or Persian cucumbers, diced
½ jalapeno pepper, minced
¼ cup cilantro, chopped
½ lime, juiced
Salt and pepper to taste

Combine all ingredients. Serve with grilled fish or fresh tortilla chips.

> ✑ Ground cherries, also known as cape gooseberries, are related to tomatillos. The outer papery husk protects the fruit inside, which looks like a yellow cherry and tastes like a sweet tomato. We stew, roast and bake them, but they are also wonderful raw, especially dipped in chocolate.

## Jerry's Tomato Salsa

Makes 3 to 4 cups

*Thanks to Jerry Burns for this recipe.*

3 large cloves garlic
1 to 3 jalapeno peppers, seeds removed
4 to 6 tomatillos, husks removed
6 meaty tomatoes, diced
1 yellow onion, finely diced
½ green Italian pepper
2 tablespoons cilantro, coarsely chopped
1 teaspoon ground cumin seed
¼ cup lime juice
½ teaspoon salt

In a food processor, finely chop garlic and jalapeno peppers. Add tomatillos and chop again. Place mixture in a large bowl, and combine with remaining ingredients. Cover and chill several hours or overnight.

For mild salsa, use 1 jalapeno pepper; for a hotter salsa, use up to 6 jalapeno peppers.

# Tomato Gratin

Serves 4 to 6

Preheat oven to 350°F.

½ cup plus 2 teaspoons olive oil
2 tablespoons basil leaves, chiffonade
½ loaf artisan bread, crust removed, bread diced
   into 1-inch pieces
Salt and pepper to taste
3 large tomatoes, sliced ½-inch thick

Purée ½ cup olive oil and basil leaves. Set aside.
In a food processor, pulse bread to make large
breadcrumbs. Toss with remaining olive oil, and
season lightly with salt and pepper. Toast on a
sheet tray until golden brown, about 10 minutes.
In a round baking dish, arrange 1 layer of sliced
tomatoes, season lightly with salt and pepper,
and repeat until all tomatoes are used. Top with
breadcrumbs, and bake 15 to 20 minutes.
Remove from oven and drizzle with basil oil.

# Pork Tenderloin with Ground Cherries

Serves 6

Preheat oven to 350°F.

2 cups ground cherries, husks removed
1 teaspoon sugar
2 pork tenderloins, about 1½ pounds each
Salt and pepper to taste
2 tablespoons grapeseed oil

In a medium saucepan, place 1 cup ground
cherries and sugar; simmer slowly to reduce by
half. Set aside.
Season pork with salt and pepper; in an oven-
proof sauté pan, heat oil and sear pork on all
sides. Add remaining ground cherries and cherry
reduction over and next to pork. Roast 15 to 20
minutes, until pork is medium rare.
Adjust seasoning if necessary. Let rest before
slicing.

# Tomatoes

## Classic Barbecue Sauce

Makes 3 cups

*Thanks to Carol Arnold for this recipe.*

2 tablespoons grapeseed oil
1 medium onion, finely chopped
3 or 4 large ripe tomatoes, finely diced (skin removed)
½ cup red wine vinegar
½ cup brown sugar, packed
2 tablespoons Worcestershire sauce
½ teaspoon salt
½ teaspoon pepper

Heat oil in a 3-quart pan over medium heat. Add onions; cook, stirring often, until soft, about 10 minutes.
Stir in tomatoes, vinegar, brown sugar, Worcestershire sauce, salt and pepper. Bring to a boil, reduce heat and simmer, uncovered, until thickened, about 1 hour. Stir occasionally to prevent sticking. When cool, cover and refrigerate. Keeps in refrigerator up to 2 weeks.

## Beef Ribs with Classic Barbecue Sauce

Serves 4

Preheat oven to 300°F.

2 racks four-bone beef ribs
2 tablespoons olive oil
Salt and pepper to taste
1 bottle dark beer

Season ribs with oil, salt and pepper. Place in a large baking dish, add beer and cover with foil. Roast 2 to 3 hours, until tender. Remove foil and brush ribs with barbecue sauce. Increase oven temperature to 350°F and roast 1 hour. Let rest at least 30 minutes before slicing and serving.

## Tomato Braised Short Ribs with Pasta

Serves 6

2 tablespoons grapeseed oil

3 pounds beef short ribs

Salt and pepper to taste

1 red onion, chopped

1 tablespoon brown sugar

1 teaspoon chili flakes

2 bay leaves

3 tablespoons lemon juice

1½ cups tomatoes, diced

1 bottle lager-style beer

1 pound whole wheat pasta

2 tablespoons parsley, chopped

In a large braising pot, heat oil. Season ribs with salt and pepper and sear on all sides. Add onions, brown sugar and spices, and cook until fragrant. Add lemon juice, tomatoes and beer. Bring to a boil, reduce heat to low, cover and simmer 2 to 2½ hours, until meat is tender. Cook pasta in boiling, salted water until tender. Drain and set aside.
Remove beef from braising jus and reduce liquid by half if desired. To serve, place ribs and jus over pasta and garnish with parsley.

## Plum and Ground Cherry Pie

Serves 8

Preheat oven to 400°F.

### Two crust pie dough for 9-inch pie

¼ cup vegetable shortening

¼ cup cold butter

1½ cups all purpose flour

½ teaspoon salt

¼ cup cold water

½ teaspoon cinnamon

½ teaspoon sugar (mix with cinnamon)

1 teaspoon Demerara sugar (optional)

Use a dough cutter to blend shortening, butter, flour and salt to cornmeal stage. Slowly add water, mixing with a fork until dough comes together. Add more water if needed. Form into a ball, cover and chill 2 hours before rolling out. Cut the dough ball into 2 pieces, one slightly larger than the other. Roll out on floured surface until ⅛-inch thick. Make dough 10 inches for bottom, and 9 inches for top. Place filling in shell. Apply top crust. Trim, roll and crimp edges. Score dough 6 or 7 places. Sprinkle top with cinnamon sugar mixture, then Demerara.

### Filling

3 cups dark red plums, sliced

2 cups ground cherries, husk removed

⅔ cup sugar

⅓ cup tapioca flour

½ teaspoon salt

1 tablespoon lemon juice

1 tablespoon cold butter

In a large bowl combine plums, ground cherries, sugar, tapioca flour, salt and lemon juice. Stir gently and let stand 20 minutes. Stir again, and spoon mixture into pie shell and place dabs of butter over fruit. Cover with remaining dough. Bake pie until juices are bubbling on the edge of the crust, about 50 minutes.

# Peaches

Seared Halibut with Tomato Peach Salsa

Roasted Pork with Peaches

Creamy Fruit Pops

Peach and Raspberry Galette

Peach Tart Tatin

*E*veryone remembers eating a just-picked perfectly ripe peach, biting into it and suddenly realizing peach juice is dripping down your chin and arm. You have just entered peach heaven.

Clingstone peaches, the ones with the flesh firmly attached to the stone, are the first peaches on the market. It's the first chance to bake with peaches, and, as nature would have it, berries and rhubarb are available at the same time for a match made in heaven. Blend peaches with another fruit, and you have a lovely pie, relish or fresh fruit toping. A drop or two of almond or vanilla extract will liven up the flavors.

Semi-freestone peaches appear on growers tables mid to late season. That's my favorite time to eat peaches. They seem to be more flavorful, and have beautiful tinges of red on the skins. The O'Henry peach is definitely worth watching and waiting for. Make pies blending late season peaches with plums, blackberries or raspberries. Wash the fuzz off the skins, but don't peel them before slicing an baking them. Pure ambrosia.

# Peaches

## Seared Halibut with Tomato Peach Salsa

Serves 6 to 8

1 tablespoon grapeseed oil
1½ to 2 pounds halibut, cut into 4 equal portions
Salt and pepper to taste

Heat oil in a large sauté pan. Season fish with salt and pepper, and sear on presentation side until golden brown and cooked about ⅔ through. Flip over; turn off pan, and let rest to finish cooking. Garnish with tomato peach salsa.

### Tomato Peach Salsa

1 cup tomatoes, chopped
½ cup peaches, chopped
2 tablespoons fresh cilantro, chopped
2 tablespoons light brown sugar
2 tablespoons lime juice
2 tablespoons grapeseed oil
Salt and pepper to taste

Combine all ingredients.

## Creamy Fruit Pops

Makes 6 frozen pops

½ cup sugar
½ cup water
2 cups fresh ripe peaches, including skins, puréed
2 tablespoons fresh lemon juice
⅓ cup Greek yogurt

Make syrup first: In a saucepan, combine sugar and water, bring to a boil and stir until sugar is dissolved. Set sugar syrup aside to cool. You can store syrup in a covered jar in the refrigerator for later use.

To make fruit pops, place peaches and lemon juice in a 2-quart bowl and purée until smooth. Blend in yogurt and 1 tablespoon sugar syrup.

Fill mold to within 1 inch of top. Freeze at least 3 hours. To remove from mold, let pops sit at room temperature 15 to 20 minutes, or run mold under warm water.

## Roasted Pork with Peaches

Serves 6

Preheat oven to 400°F.

2 cloves garlic, minced
2 tablespoons basil, chopped
2 tablespoons olive oil
Salt and pepper to taste
1 pork shoulder, 2 to 2½ pounds
3 peaches, pitted and sliced

Combine garlic, basil, oil, salt and pepper in small bowl. Rub liberally over pork and marinate 20 to 25 minutes.

Roast 20 minutes, then reduce oven temperature to 325°F and continue to cook 60 to 90 minutes, depending on the size. Let meat rest before slicing; arrange on a large platter with peach slices.

> ℰ᷉ Substitute two cups of other puréed fruits for a bowl full of colors and flavors: strawberries, blueberries, raspberries or blackberries (strained to take out seeds).

# Peaches

## Peach and Raspberry Galette

Serves 6 to 8

Preheat oven to 400°F.

### Galette dough for 9-inch pie pan

3 tablespoons vegetable shortening
3 tablespoons cold butter
1 cup all purpose flour
¼ teaspoon salt
3 tablespoons cold water
½ teaspoon cinnamon
½ teaspoon sugar (mix with cinnamon)
½ teaspoon Demerara sugar (optional)

Use a pie dough cutter to blend shortening, butter, flour and salt to cornmeal stage. Slowly add cold water, mixing with a fork until dough comes together. Add more water if necessary. Form into a ball, cover and chill at least 2 hours before rolling out.

In the palm of your hand, form ball into round flat disk. Roll dough on a floured surface until it is ⅛-inch thick. Dough will be 14 to16 inches in diameter. Place in bottom of 9-inch pie pan; dough will fall over edges of pan. Set aside.

Late-crop peaches are sweeter and juicier than early summer peaches. I prefer waiting until these peaches are available before baking a pie or galette. If baking with my favorite peach, the O'Henry, I use raspberries from the freezer or wild blackberries in the recipe.

### Filling

2 cups peaches, sliced
2 cups raspberries
½ cup sugar
¼ cup tapioca flour
½ teaspoon salt
1 teaspoon almond extract
1 tablespoon cold butter

In a large bowl place peaches, raspberries, sugar, tapioca flour, salt and almond extract. Stir gently and let stand 20 minutes.

Stir again, and spoon mixture into center of galette shell, and distribute small pieces of butter over fruit.

Bring edges of dough toward the center over fruit and staple to fruit with toothpicks. There will be a small opening in the middle. Sprinkle top of crust with cinnamon sugar, then Demerara.

Bake until a toothpick inserted comes out clean and juices are bubbling around the crust, 45 to 50 minutes.

# Peach Tart Tatin

Serves 6

Preheat oven to 375°F.

1¼ cups flour
1 teaspoon plus ¾ cup sugar
¾ teaspoon salt
6 tablespoons cold butter
1 egg, beaten
1 tablespoon cold water
½ cup butter
4 to 5 peaches, halved and pitted
¼ cup crème fraîche

In a food processor, combine flour, 1 teaspoon sugar, salt and 6 tablespoons cold butter until mixture resembles coarse cornmeal. While machine is running, slowly add egg and water and pulse until just combined.

Turn dough onto work surface and form into a ball. Wrap with plastic and refrigerate 1 hour. Between 2 pieces of parchment paper, roll dough into a circle, about 11 inches wide and ⅛-inch thick. Cover and refrigerate 1 hour.

Melt ½ cup butter in a large cast iron pan over medium low heat. Stir in remaining sugar and continue cooking until dissolved and lightly caramelized, about 10 minutes. Remove pan from heat and arrange peaches in pan, cut side up. Let cool 2 to 3 minutes. Take dough from refrigerator, and score it in 6 or 7 places to allow air to vent. Cover peaches with dough, and tuck around the edges. Bake 25 to 30 minutes, until golden brown.

Run a knife around the edges to loosen, and then flip onto a large plate. Garnish with crème fraîche.

# July 30

# Corn

Corn Tortillas

Corn and Cherry Tomato Relish

Corn and Jalapeno Sauce

Quinoa Corn Cakes with Lemon Dill Sauce and Baharat Spice

Summer time means corn makes its way to the table in one form or another. We enjoy salad made with raw shaved corn, but the question of how to cook corn on the cob comes up often. I prefer to grill it in the husk; I like the smoky flavor grilling imparts. If time is an issue, or the weather inclement, I gently boil the shucked cobs in salted water. We advise transferring other vegetables to an ice bath after par boiling, but in this case, don't! Submerging cooked corn in ice water will make it soggy. A standard garnish in my house is a light layer of chili powder and mayo, with a sprinkling of Cotijas cheese.

## Corn Tortillas

Serves 4

1 cup masa harina
2 teaspoons salt
⅔ cup water

In a small bowl, combine all ingredients with a fork. Mix well until consistency of dough. Divide dough into 1 to 2 tablespoon size balls, and flatten in a tortilla press. Cook over medium heat in a dry sauté pan, about 45 seconds per side.

# Corn

## Corn and Cherry Tomato Relish

Serves 4

1 pint cherry tomatoes, halved
2 ears corn, shucked, kernels removed
2 green peppers, roasted and diced
1 tablespoon olive oil
Salt and pepper to taste

Combine all ingredients and season to taste with salt and pepper.

## Corn and Jalapeno Sauce

Serves 4

Preheat oven to 350°F.

2 ears corn, shucked
1 jalapeno pepper
1 teaspoon olive oil
1 tablespoon butter
½ cup diced yellow onion
Salt and pepper to taste

Remove corn kernels from cob and set aside.
To make corn stock, place cobs in a medium pot and add enough water to barely cover. Bring to a boil. Reduce heat and simmer 30 to 40 minutes. Strain and discard cobs. Set stock aside.
Coat jalapeno with oil; roast 15 to 20 minutes.
Heat butter in a medium sauté pan and add onions. Cook until fragrant. Add corn kernels and season lightly with salt and pepper.
In a food processor, purée corn and half of the jalapeno. Add more jalapeno if you like it spicier. Add ¼ cup corn stock and continue to purée. If too thick, add more stock. Add salt and pepper to taste.
Serve as a dipping sauce with grilled prawns.
Extra corn stock keeps up to 2 weeks in refrigerator.

# Quinoa Corn Cakes with Lemon Dill Sauce and Baharat Spice

Serves 4

1½ cups cooked quinoa

2 cloves garlic

2 tablespoons red onion, chopped

¼ cup carrots, grated

½ cup spinach, thinly sliced

½ cup corn, sliced from cob

1 tablespoon lemon zest

1 tablespoon lemon juice

2 eggs, whisked

⅓ cup panko breadcrumbs

Salt and pepper to taste

1 tablespoon Baharat spice

1 tablespoon grapeseed oil

In a medium bowl combine quinoa, garlic, onions, carrots, spinach, corn, zest and juice. Mix well.

Add eggs and enough breadcrumbs so mixture is sticky. Add salt and pepper to taste; add Baharat spice. Set aside.

Heat oil in cast iron pan. Make quinoa mixture into patties in the palm of your hand. Carefully place in warm oil. Fill the pan with patties and cook 5 to 7 minutes each side. Corn cakes taste best when cooked to golden brown with crunchy edges. Serve with lemon dill sauce.

> Use a spatter guard when frying the quinoa corn cakes to prevent eye and skin injuries. Heat causes the water inside a kernel of corn to expand and pop.

## Lemon Dill Sauce

2 tablespoons fresh dill, chopped

1 lemon, juiced

2 tablespoons lemon zest

1 cup plain yogurt

¼ cup mayonnaise

Mix together and serve on the side.

> Used in Middle Eastern cooking; baharat spice is available at Middle Eastern markets. This blend keeps well for 6 months.

## Baharat Spice

¼ cup ground black pepper

¼ cup paprika

3 tablespoons ground cumin

2 tablespoons ground cloves

2 tablespoons ground cinnamon

2 tablespoons ground coriander

4 teaspoons ground nutmeg

1 teaspoon ground cardamom

Combine all ingredients until mixed well. Store in an airtight container out of direct light.

# Blackberries

Romaine Salad with Blackberry Vinaigrette

Wild Blackberry and Rhubarb Cobbler

Wild Blackberry and Rhubarb Galette

Wild Blackberry and Pear Galette

Wild Blackberry and Plum Galette

Blackberry Crisp

Cheesecake with Graham Cracker Crust

Growing up, I remember my mother tying the handle of a one-quart Karo syrup pail to my jeans and then pointing me in the direction of the ripe wild raspberries. My job was to pick enough for a wild berry pie. In Minnesota the wild raspberry is called a black cap. Once you taste a black cap, the flavor and texture are firmly planted in your brain. Your taste buds never forget.

A few years ago we discovered wild blackberries close to home. Wild blackberries ripen later than domestic blackberries. The taste is so amazing we patiently wait until the berries turn a deep, rich color. Only then is the flavor fully developed. Of course, you have to beat the birds to the blackberry patch. We visit the patch several times over a three to four week period, picking berries each time. We manage to freeze several gallons of them to enjoy throughout the winter and spring.

Blackberries are high in dietary fiber, vitamin C, vitamin K, folic acid, and the essential mineral manganese. The seeds contain oil rich in Omega-3 and linoleic acid. Blackberries are at the top of more than 1,000 antioxidant foods consumed in the U.S.

# Blackberries

## Romaine Salad with Blackberry Vinaigrette

Serves 8

1 head romaine lettuce, torn into 1-inch pieces
2 ounces blue cheese, crumbled
¼ cup pecans, toasted
½ cup blackberries

### Blackberry Vinaigrette

1 cup blackberries
¼ cup olive oil
2 tablespoons Champagne vinegar
Salt and pepper to taste

Toss salad ingredients together.
Purée 1 cup blackberries until smooth; strain out seeds if desired. Whisk in oil and vinegar; season to taste with salt and pepper. Add to salad just before serving.

> ☙ The best time to stock up on raspberries, blackberries and boysenberries is when they are in season. That's when their nutritional value is the highest. To freeze them, cover a sheet tray with parchment paper and spread the berries on the paper in a single layer. Don't wash them. Put the tray in the freezer over night. Store fully frozen berries in plastic tubs or freezer bags.

## Wild Blackberry and Rhubarb Cobbler

Serves 8

Preheat oven to 375°F.

### Filling

4 cups wild blackberries
4 cups rhubarb, cut into ½-inch slices
1 cup sugar
⅓ cup tapioca flour
1 tablespoon lemon juice
1 teaspoon lemon zest
1 teaspoon vanilla
Pinch of salt

Combine all ingredients and let stand 20 minutes before transferring to a buttered 3-quart baking dish.

### Topping

1 cup all purpose flour
1 cup walnuts, chopped
1 cup sugar
½ teaspoon baking powder
½ teaspoon salt
½ cup cold butter, cubed
1 egg, beaten

Mix together flour, walnuts, sugar, baking powder and salt.
Cut in butter with pastry blender or fork. Knead with fingertips until mixture resembles coarse sand.
Blend in egg; arrange topping over berries in clumps, covering evenly.
Bake until golden brown and bubbly, 40 to 45 minutes.

# Wild Blackberry and Rhubarb Galette

Serves 6 to 8

Preheat oven to 400°F.

## Galette dough for 9-inch pie pan

3 tablespoons vegetable shortening

3 tablespoons butter

1 cup all purpose flour

2 tablespoons cold water

1 teaspoon cinnamon

1 teaspoon sugar (mix with cinnamon)

½ teaspoon Demerara sugar (optional)


Use a pie dough cutter to blend shortening, butter, flour and salt to cornmeal stage. Slowly add cold water, mixing with a fork until dough comes together. Add more water if necessary. Form into a ball, cover and chill at least 2 hours before rolling out.

In the palm of your hand, form ball into round flat disk. Roll dough on a floured surface until it is ⅛-inch thick. Dough will be 14 to16 inches in diameter. Place in bottom of 9-inch pie pan; dough will fall over edges of pan.

## Filling

2 cups wild blackberries

2½ cups rhubarb, sliced into ½-inch pieces

⅔ cup sugar

⅓ cup tapioca flour

½ teaspoon salt

1 teaspoon almond extract

1 tablespoon butter


In a medium bowl, blend together fruit, sugar, tapioca flour, salt, and almond extract. Stir gently and let stand 20 minutes.

Stir again, and spoon mixture into center of galette shell and distribute small pieces of butter over the fruit.

Bring edges of dough toward the center over fruit and staple to fruit with toothpicks. There will be a small opening in the middle. Sprinkle top of crust with cinnamon sugar, then Demerara.

Bake until a toothpick inserted comes out clean and juices are bubbling around the crust, 45 to 50 minutes.

# Blackberries

## Wild Blackberry and Pear Galette

Serves 6 to 8

Preheat oven to 400°F.

### Galette dough for 9-inch pie pan
3 tablespoons vegetable shortening
3 tablespoons butter
1 cup all purpose flour
2 tablespoons cold water
1 teaspoon cinnamon
1 teaspoon sugar (mix with cinnamon)
½ teaspoon Demerara sugar (optional)

Use a pie dough cutter to blend shortening, butter, flour and salt to cornmeal stage. Slowly add cold water, mixing with a fork until dough comes together. Add more water if necessary. Form into a ball, cover and chill at least 2 hours before rolling out.
In the palm of your hand, form ball into round flat disk. Roll dough on a floured surface until it is ⅛-inch thick. Dough will be 14 to16 inches in diameter. Place in bottom of 9-inch pie pan; dough will fall over edges of pan.

### Filling
2 cups wild blackberries
2½ cups sliced pears
⅔ cup sugar
⅓ cup tapioca flour
1 teaspoon almond extract
1 tablespoon butter

In a medium bowl, blend together fruit, sugar, tapioca flour, salt, and almond extract. Stir gently and let stand 20 minutes.
Stir again, and spoon fruit mixture into center of the galette shell. Distribute small pieces of butter evenly over fruit.
Bring edges of dough toward the center over fruit and staple to fruit with toothpicks. There will be a small opening in the middle. Sprinkle top of crust with cinnamon sugar, then Demerara.
Bake until a toothpick inserted comes out clean and juices are bubbling around the crust, 45 to 50 minutes.

# Wild Blackberry and Plum Galette

Serves 6 to 8

Preheat oven to 400°F.

## Galette dough for 9-inch pie pan

3 tablespoons vegetable shortening
3 tablespoons butter
1 cup all purpose flour
2 tablespoons cold water
1 teaspoon cinnamon
1 teaspoon sugar (mix with cinnamon)
½ teaspoon Demerara sugar (optional)

Use a pie dough cutter to blend shortening, butter, flour and salt to cornmeal stage. Slowly add cold water, mixing with a fork, until dough comes together. Add more water if necessary. Form into a ball, cover and chill at least 2 hours before rolling out.

In the palm of your hand, form ball into round flat disk. Roll dough on a floured surface until it is ⅛-inch thick. Dough will be 14 to16 inches in diameter. Place in bottom of 9-inch pie pan; dough will fall over edges of pan.

## Filling

2 cups wild blackberries
2½ cups sliced plums
⅔ cup sugar
⅓ cup tapioca flour
1 teaspoon almond extract
1 tablespoon butter

In a medium bowl, blend together fruit, sugar, tapioca flour, salt, and almond extract. Stir gently and let stand 20 minutes.

Stir again, and spoon fruit mixture into center of galette shell. Distribute small pieces of butter evenly over fruit.

Bring edges of dough toward the center over fruit and staple to fruit with toothpicks. There will be a small opening in the middle. Sprinkle top of crust with cinnamon sugar, then Demerara.

Bake until a toothpick inserted comes out clean and juices are bubbling around the crust, 45 to 50 minutes.

# Blackberries

*If you're not hungry enough to eat an apple, then you're probably not hungry.*
*—Michael Pollan*

## Blackberry Crisp

Serves 6 to 8

Preheat oven to 375°F.

6 cups blackberries, wild or domestic
⅓ cup sugar
1 teaspoon almond extract
1 cup oats
½ cup brown sugar
¼ cup flour
½ teaspoon salt
¼ cup butter

Combine blackberries, sugar and almond extract. Place in a buttered 9x13-inch baking dish. Set aside.

Combine oats, brown sugar, flour, and salt in a mixing bowl. Cut in butter until well mixed. Place the topping over blackberries and bake until golden brown, about 30 to 35 minutes. Serve warm or at room temperature.

# Cheesecake with Graham Cracker Crust

Serves 10 to 12

*Thanks to Theresa Duggan for this recipe.*

Preheat oven to 350°F.

## Graham Cracker Crust

10 graham crackers, crushed
⅓ cup sugar
½ cup butter, melted

Mix all ingredients until well blended.
Press firmly onto bottom and up sides of a
10-inch spring form pan.
Bake 8 to 10 minutes, or until lightly browned.
Cool completely.

## Filling

Preheat oven to 325°F.

24 ounces Gina Marie cream cheese
½ cup sugar
4 large eggs
16 ounces sour cream
1 teaspoon vanilla

In a mixing bowl blend cream cheese, sugar,
eggs (1 at a time), sour cream, and vanilla. Pour
mixture into cooled crust and bake 35 minutes.
Cool 1 hour; refrigerate at least 4 hours before
serving.
Serve cheesecake plain, or with a fresh fruit
topping.

# Pink-Eyed Peas

Artichokes with Balsamic Reduction

Pink–Eyed Pea Succotash

Herbed Pink–Eyed Peas with Halibut Cheeks

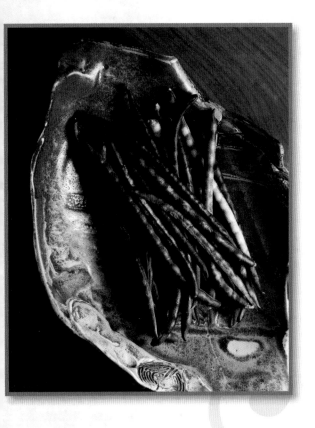

*I*t's a nice surprise to discover a big basket of pink-eyed peas on a growers table. I immediately think about the many tasty ways to serve this beautiful vegetable. We always pack our basket with enough pink-eyed peas for several meals because once you start shucking the peas, you might as well shuck enough for two or three meals. Shucked peas freeze well and can be prepared at a later date so when you find pink-eyed peas, buy enough for future meals.

Pink-eyed peas, or cowpeas, definitely attract attention. The pods are colorful – every shade of pink, from light to very dark with tinges of burgundy. Select long pods that are full sized and firm, but make sure they are not beginning to dry.

Pink-eyed peas are tasty in a salad with plenty of herbs and mild onions, and great cooked with pork. Pork and beans go together, and fresh peas take the art of eating pink-eyed or black-eyed peas to the next level.

# Pink-Eyed Peas

## Artichokes with Balsamic Reduction

Serves 4

2 tablespoons balsamic vinegar
1 tablespoon pickling spices
¼ cup olive oil
Salt and pepper to taste
4 artichokes, stems and thorns trimmed
1 tablespoon butter

Combine vinegar, spices and oil and season lightly with salt and pepper. Place artichokes stem side down in a large stainless steel skillet. Drizzle vinegar mixture over top and between the leaves of the artichokes. Add 1 to 2 inches of water to pan, cover and bring to a boil. Reduce heat and simmer 45 to 60 minutes, until knife tender. Remove from pan and drain upside down on a paper towel.

Strain and reduce braising liquid to ⅓ cup. Stir in butter and season to taste with salt and pepper. Serve artichokes whole, using balsamic reduction as dipping sauce.

## Pink-Eyed Pea Succotash

Serves 4 to 6

2 tablespoons grapeseed oil
½ onion, small diced
1 clove garlic, minced
3 stalks celery, halved
1 pound pink-eyed peas, shucked
Salt and pepper to taste
1 tablespoon butter
1 bunch baby carrots, peeled and sliced
  ½-inch thick
1 ear corn, shucked and kernels removed
½ pound Romano beans, sliced into ½-inch pieces
2 tablespoons chives, diced

In a medium pot, heat oil and cook onion, garlic and celery until fragrant. Add peas and enough water to cover. Bring to a boil and turn down to simmer until peas are tender, about 1 hour. After peas are cooked, drain excess water, and discard celery. Season to taste with salt and pepper. Set aside.

In a large sauté pan, heat butter and add carrots. Quickly cook over high heat, about 2 to 4 minutes, and season to taste with salt and pepper. Remove from pan and repeat process for corn (cook 1 minute) and Romano beans (cook 2 minutes). Toss all vegetables with cooked peas and garnish with chives.

# Herbed Pink-Eyed Peas
# with Halibut Cheeks

Serves 6

2 tablespoons grapeseed oil
½ onion, small diced
1 clove garlic, minced
1 pound pink-eyed peas, shucked
Salt and pepper to taste
1 bunch basil
½ bunch parsley
1 tablespoon olive oil
1 teaspoon butter, softened
2 pounds halibut cheeks
1 lemon

In a medium pot, heat 1 tablespoon grapeseed oil, and cook onions and garlic until fragrant. Add peas and enough water to cover. Bring to a boil and turn down to simmer until peas are tender, about 1 hour. Drain; season to taste with salt and pepper. Set aside.

Blanch basil and parsley in a small pot of boiling, salted water for 30 seconds, and then immediately transfer to an ice bath. When cool, remove from water and squeeze to release excess water. Place in food processor and purée with olive oil until smooth. Gently stir herb mixture and butter into peas.
To cook halibut cheeks, heat remaining grapeseed oil over high heat. Season cheeks with salt and pepper and sear quickly on both sides. Be careful not to overcook.
Serve halibut on bed of peas. Squeeze lemon juice over top.

*Limit your snacks to unprocessed plant foods.*
*–Michael Pollan*

# Green Beans

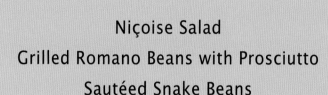

Niçoise Salad
Grilled Romano Beans with Prosciutto
Sautéed Snake Beans
Chocolate Ganache Cake

## Niçoise Salad

Serves 4 to 6

2 tablespoons olive oil
1 tablespoon Champagne vinegar
Salt and pepper to taste
1½ pounds small potatoes, boiled
  until tender, and halved
½ pound Romano beans, blanched
6 Juliette tomatoes, halved
3 small eggs, hard boiled, peeled, then halved
4 ounces canned tuna
½ cup Niçoise olives

Combine oil and vinegar and season to taste with
salt and pepper. Toss potatoes with ⅓ of oil
mixture. Set aside. Repeat with beans and
tomatoes.
Arrange potatoes, beans, tomatoes, eggs and
tuna on platter, and garnish with olives.
(If using fresh tuna, cut into 2-inch pieces,
season with oil, salt and pepper. Preheat oven to
350°F and bake 10 to 15 minutes, until flaky.)

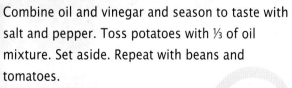

# Green Beans

## Grilled Romano Beans with Prosciutto

Serves 6

Preheat grill.

2 pounds Romano beans
1 tablespoon olive oil
Salt and pepper to taste
1 lemon, juiced
¼ pound prosciutto, torn into pieces

Season beans with oil, salt and pepper. Grill on medium high heat until tender. Place in a bowl, add remaining ingredients, and add more salt and pepper if desired.
This is a perfect accompaniment to grilled steak or roasted chicken.

## Sautéed Snake Beans

Serves 6

1 tablespoon olive oil
1 tablespoon butter
1 clove garlic, minced
1½ pound snake beans
Salt and pepper to taste

Heat oil and butter in a large sauté pan. Add garlic and cook until fragrant. Add beans and cook 1 to 1½ minutes, until "squeaky". Season to taste with salt and pepper.

You know your green beans are cooked when they squeak as you bite down on them. The friction between your teeth and the somewhat tough skin of the bean make a slight squeaking noise, which lets you know that you have not softened the skin too much by overcooking them.

It's not your imagination. Chocolate really does make you feel good. It contains tryptophan, an essential amino acid the body needs to produce serotonin, a neurotransmitter that regulates appetite, sleep and mood. By boosting serotonin levels, chocolate generates feelings of well-being and curbs anxiety and depression. Other serotonin boosting (tryptophan-rich) foods include red meat, seafood, turkey, milk products, nuts, seeds, beans and bananas.

# Chocolate Ganache Cake

Serves 6 to 8

Preheat oven to 350°F.

¾ cup boiling water
½ cup Sweet Earth orange cocoa
2 teaspoons instant espresso powder
½ cup whole milk
1 teaspoon vanilla
2 cups all purpose flour
1¼ teaspoons baking soda
¼ teaspoon salt
1 cup (2 sticks) unsalted butter, room temperature
1¾ cups dark brown sugar, packed
4 large eggs

Whisk together water, orange cocoa, and espresso powder until smooth, then add milk and vanilla. Set aside.

Sift together flour, baking soda, and salt. Set aside. Place butter and brown sugar in bowl; mix at high speed until fluffy. Add eggs, one at a time, and beat after each addition. Add small amounts of flour and cocoa mixture alternately until all used. Make sure all ingredients are thoroughly blended. Line a 13x9-inch baking pan with parchment paper. Butter parchment paper and sides of pan. Pour batter into baking pan. Bake on middle rack of oven 30 to 35 minutes, until toothpick comes out clean. Cool pan on a rack.
Spread ganache topping over cake when cool.

## Ganache Topping

1¼ cups heavy cream
10 ounces Sweet Earth bittersweet
   chocolate chips

Place cream in a 2-quart saucepan. When cream simmers, remove from heat. Whisk in chocolate chips until smooth. Pour into a bowl, and refrigerate, stirring once or twice until ganache thickens, 3½ to 4 hours. If ganache is too thick, let stand at room temperature. Spread ganache over cake. Chill. Slice into small squares to serve.

We used Sweet Earth bittersweet chocolate chips (65%) and organic orange cocoa in this recipe. Their chocolate is organic, fair traded and made in the USA. Visit www.sweetearthchocolates.com.

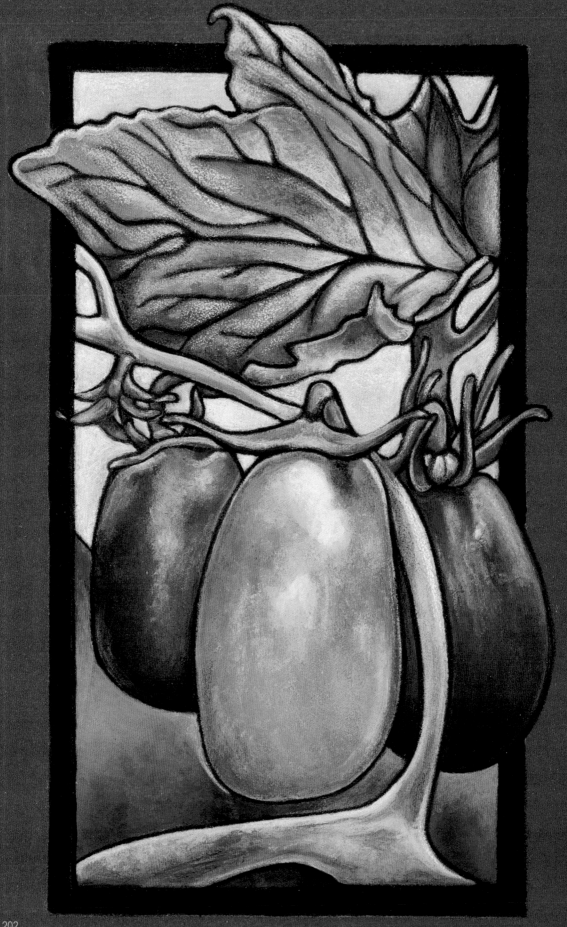

# Roma Tomatoes

Blue Cheese Stuffed Juliette Tomatoes
Beef Stir Fry with Tomatoes
Penne Pasta with Tomatoes, Fennel and Peppers
Roasted Chicken with Tomatoes, Green Beans and Mushrooms

## Blue Cheese Stuffed Juliette Tomatoes

Serves 4 to 6

4 ounces Pt. Reyes blue cheese
2 tablespoons crème fraîche
Salt and pepper to taste
8 Juliette tomatoes, halved lengthwise
Chives, for garnish

Mix together cheese and crème fraîche until well combined. Add salt and pepper to taste. Carefully remove seeds from tomatoes and stuff with cheese mixture. Garnish with chives.

# Roma Tomatoes

## Beef Stir Fry with Tomatoes

Serves 4 to 6

1 cup soy sauce

1 cup mirin

3 tablespoons sugar

1 tablespoon ginger, peeled and sliced

Cornstarch slurry, if needed

2 tablespoons grapeseed oil

1½ pounds flank steak, thinly sliced

1 bunch Chinese long beans, cut into
    2-inch pieces

4 large tomatoes, cut into wedges

2 cups brown rice, cooked

In a small saucepan, heat soy sauce, mirin, sugar
and ginger over medium high heat. Bring to a
boil and reduce to simmer about 20 minutes.
Add salt and pepper to taste, and thicken if
needed with cornstarch slurry*. Set aside.
In a large sauté pan, heat oil and quickly sear
flank steak over high heat. Remove from pan into
a large bowl. Add beans to pan and cook until
tender, about 1 minute; add to bowl with beef.
Toss with sauce and tomatoes and serve over
brown rice.

*Make a cornstarch slurry by whisking one
tablespoon corn starch into ½ cup water. Add
a little at a time to the saucepan; bring liquid
to a boil to check thickness. Repeat if
necessary until mixture is desired thickness.*

## Penne Pasta with Tomatoes, Fennel and Peppers

Serves 4

1 pound whole wheat penne pasta

1 tablespoon olive oil

1 tablespoon butter

1 large fennel bulb, julienne

2 medium peppers, julienne

3 large tomatoes, diced

3 tablespoons scallions, sliced

Salt and pepper to taste

Cook pasta in boiling, salted water until tender.
Drain and set aside.
Heat oil and butter in a large sauté pan and add
fennel; cook until fragrant. Add peppers and
cook 2 minutes. Add cooked pasta to vegetables
and toss with tomatoes and scallions. Season to
taste with salt and pepper.

The chicken sold at the farmers
market are generally larger than ones from a
typical grocery store. The breasts are smaller
(as they grow naturally), but the body is
larger. We usually serve 4 people with one
chicken.

# Roasted Chicken with Tomatoes, Green Beans and Mushrooms

Serves 4

Preheat oven to 350°F.

1 whole chicken, 2 to 3 pounds
1 tablespoon olive oil
Salt and pepper to taste
1 lemon, halved
2 sprigs thyme
¼ bunch parsley
1 pint cherry tomatoes
3 tablespoons grapeseed oil
½ pound mushrooms
2 cloves garlic, minced
½ pound green beans

Season chicken with olive oil, salt and pepper and stuff the cavity with lemon and herbs. Roast 1 to 1½ hours, until legs are loose and juices run clear.

Toss tomatoes with 1 tablespoon grapeseed oil, salt and pepper. Roast on a sheet tray 10 to 15 minutes. Remove and set aside.

In a large sauté pan, heat 1 tablespoon grapeseed oil and cook mushrooms until they begin to caramelize. Add garlic and continue to cook until fragrant. Remove from pan.

Heat remaining grapeseed oil and sauté green beans until just tender. Combine with tomatoes and mushrooms.

To serve, cut chicken into six pieces and serve with sautéed vegetables.

> This recipe is a perfect illustration of using seasonal ingredients to create a simple and delicious dinner. Use the basic method of roasting a chicken and add whatever is in your refrigerator and in season.

*September 3*

# Melons

Mixed Melon Salad

Polenta Panzanella Salad with Melon and Cucumber

Miso Crusted Black Cod

Pistachio Ice Cream Balls

## Mixed Melon Salad

Serves 4

4 cups summer melons, large diced

¼ cup feta cheese, crumbled

2 tablespoons mint, chiffonade

2 tablespoons almonds, chopped

1 tablespoon olive oil

Salt to taste

Arrange melon on a large platter and garnish with remaining ingredients.

# Polenta Panzanella Salad with Melon and Cucumber

Serves 6

Preheat oven to 375°F.

3½ cups chicken or vegetable stock

1 cup polenta

¼ cup asiago cheese

3 tablespoons butter

Salt and pepper to taste

1 tablespoon olive oil

1 cup zucchini, small diced

1 lemon, zest and juice

½ cup melon, peeled and diced into ¼-inch pieces

½ cup cucumber, diced into ¼-inch pieces

¼ cup basil, chiffonade

In a medium pot, heat stock and add polenta. Cook over medium low heat, stirring frequently, until tender, about 30 minutes. Stir in cheese and 1 tablespoon butter, and season to taste with salt and pepper. Immediately spread mixture evenly over sheet tray. Refrigerate until completely cool. Cut cooled polenta into 1-inch squares and coat lightly with oil. Place in oven and toast until edges begin to brown, about 15 minutes.

Heat remaining butter in sauté pan and cook zucchini until slightly browned. Place in a large bowl with lemon, melon, cucumber and toasted polenta. Stir in basil and season to taste with salt and pepper.

This salad is delicious served with seared fish.

Lifestyles are rapidly changing, but for many Japanese the day still begins with a bowl of miso soup. Miso is a preserve of salt fermented with grains and beans. Many kinds of miso are available in United States supermarkets. They are categorized into three grades depending on strength and color: white, red and black. We prefer white miso, which is light in flavor and made with rice.

Mirin is an amber-colored sweetened sake used in cooking. Look for mirin with a 14% alcohol content. Mirin has a faint sake aroma and syrupy texture that adds sweetness and a shiny glaze to food. It's used in simmered dishes and in glazing sauces.

Stored in a tightly covered jar in the refrigerator, both will keep a long time.

# Miso Crusted Black Cod

Serves 2 to 4

*Thanks to Roz Seid for this recipe.*

Preheat oven to broil.

¼ cup miso
1 tablespoon fresh ginger, grated
1 tablespoon sugar
2 tablespoons mirin and 2 tablespoons water
   (No mirin? Use ¼ cup water)
2 eight-ounce pieces of black cod

Mix together miso, ginger, sugar and mirin water. Marinate cod 30 to 60 minutes. Broil fish flesh side down to golden brown. Reduce heat to 350°F and roast until done, about 10 minutes per inch of thickness of fish.

# Pistachio Ice Cream Balls

Serves 4

1 quart vanilla ice cream
¼ cup unsalted pistachios, finely diced
¼ cup graham cracker crumbs
2 cups cantaloupe, sliced into ½-inch pieces
1 cup blackberries
Fresh mint for garnish

Remove ice cream from freezer and hold at room temperature 5 minutes so it can be easily scooped.

Blend pistachios and cracker crumbs. Roll 4 balls of ice cream in nut mixture. Place on parchment lined pan. Immediately place in freezer.

Mix cantaloupe and blackberries together. Serve in sauce dishes; top each with an ice cream ball and garnish with fresh mint.

*September 10*

# Grapes

❧

Grilled Grapes with Brie Cheese

Halibut Croquettes with Tartar Sauce

Pan Seared Salmon with Grape Salsa

Pork Chops with Grapes and Blue Cheese

Autumn Raisin and Nut Cake

## Grilled Grapes with Brie Cheese

Serves 4

Preheat grill.

1 four-ounce round brie cheese, cut into
  quarter wedges
4 small bunches grapes
1 loaf artisan bread, cut into ½-inch slices
1 jar pomegranate jelly

Coat clean hot grill with olive oil to prevent
sticking. Grill brie on both rind sides, about 1
minute, until grill marks appear. Remove and set
aside. Repeat process with bunches of grapes.
Brush bread with oil and grill. Arrange brie,
grapes and bread on a serving plate. Serve as an
appetizer with pomegranate jelly.

# Halibut Croquettes with Tartar Sauce

Serves 4

1 pound halibut
1 tablespoon grapeseed oil
2 cups mashed potatoes
1 tablespoon dill, chopped
Salt and pepper to taste
1 cup flour, seasoned with salt and pepper
2 eggs, beaten
2 cups panko breadcrumbs
2 tablespoons grapeseed oil

Sear fish in large sauté pan with oil. Shred fish and place in a large bowl with potatoes and dill. Season to taste with salt and pepper.
Divide into 8 equal portions and round out to disk-shaped, compressing slightly. Place flour, egg and panko in three separate bowls. Coat each croquette in flour, then egg, then panko. Heat oil in a large sauté pan and fry croquettes on both sides until golden brown. Serve warm with tartar sauce.

## Tartar Sauce

1 cup mayonnaise
½ cup sour cream
1 lemon, juiced
1 tablespoon capers, rinsed and chopped
1 tablespoon parsley, chopped
Salt, pepper and cayenne to taste

Combine all ingredients and season to taste with salt, pepper and cayenne.

> This recipe is a delicious way to use leftover mashed potatoes.

# Pan Seared Salmon with Grape Salsa

Serves 4

½ cup grapes, halved
¼ cup chopped walnuts, toasted
1 tablespoon lemon zest
1 tablespoon mint, chiffonade
2 tablespoons olive oil
Salt and pepper to taste
2 tablespoons grapeseed oil
1 pound salmon, cut into 4 portions

To make salsa, combine grapes, walnuts, lemon zest, mint and olive oil. Season to taste with salt and pepper; set aside.

Heat grapeseed oil in a large sauté pan. Season salmon with salt and pepper and sear on presentation side until cooked ⅓ through. Flip fish, and continue to cook 30 seconds longer, depending on thickness. Turn off heat and let finish in pan.

To serve, place salmon on a large platter and top with grape salsa.

# Grapes

## Pork Chops with Grapes and Blue Cheese

Serves 4

*This recipe was inspired by Jennifer Elliott.*

Preheat grill.

2 tablespoons butter
2 onions, julienne
4 pork chops
1 tablespoon olive oil
Salt and pepper to taste
2 ounces Pt. Reyes blue cheese, crumbled
1 pear, thinly sliced
1 cup grapes, halved

Heat butter in a large sauté pan and cook onions over medium heat until well caramelized, 20 to 25 minutes, stirring frequently.

Season pork chops with oil, salt and pepper and grill until marked on both sides and cooked ⅔ through. Remove from grill, and top with blue cheese.

Place warm pork chops on a platter on top of caramelized onions. Garnish with pears and grapes.

# Autumn Raisin and Nut Cake

Serves 18

Preheat oven to 350°F.

1 cup mixed raisins

1 cup fresh orange or mandarin juice

½ cup butter, room temperature

¼ cup granulated sugar

½ cup brown sugar

2 eggs

½ cup applesauce

1 teaspoon orange or mandarin zest

1½ cups flour, sifted

2 teaspoons cinnamon

1 teaspoon nutmeg

1 teaspoon soda

1 teaspoon baking powder

½ teaspoon salt

⅔ cup walnuts or pecans, chopped

In a small sauce pan, cover raisins with orange juice and bring to a boil; turn off stove and remove from heat; let cool. Drain, and save orange water. Set aside raisins and orange water.

In a large bowl, whip butter and sugars until fluffy; add eggs and mix.

Add applesauce, ¼ cup orange water, zest and blend.

Add flour, cinnamon, nutmeg, soda, baking powder and salt.

Fold in raisins and nuts until blended.

Bake in a buttered 13x 9-inch baking pan 45 to 50 minutes.

To serve, dust with powdered sugar, or spoon a dollop of crème fraîche on each serving. For a sweeter option, spread 1 cup semisweet chocolate chips over cake before baking.

The raisin and nut cake was inspired by my Aunt Delores Krinke's late 1940s, early 1950s recipe. Her daughter Mariann Krinke Ostbye remembers the recipe with mouth-watering affection. She also fondly remembers – with her brother – cutting and eating the cake before it was cool.

For a little zip I added mandarin zest to the original recipe.

# Green Tomatoes, Cherry Tomatoes & Tomatillos

Roasted Pepper and Tomato Salsa

Fried Green Tomatoes with Roasted Red Bell Pepper Aioli

Chili Verde

Green Tomato and Tarragon Chicken

Spaghetti Sauce with Wild Meat

Our local farmers market has a vendor who roasts peppers in a barrel-shaped, rotisserie-type grill. We can always tell when peppers are roasting by the sweet but smoky aroma that fills the market air. The prepared product is not only delicious, but saves us a little prep time in the kitchen.

To roast peppers, we prefer to use a wood-fired grill, which is time-consuming. As an alternative, the peppers can be roasted directly on a gas grill or burner until the skin chars. Then place them in a sealed bowl to steam the skin away from the flesh of the pepper.

## Roasted Pepper and Tomato Salsa

Serves 4 to 6

3 Anaheim peppers, roasted, small diced
1 basket cherry tomatoes, halved
2 ears fresh corn, shucked, kernels removed
1 teaspoon cumin
Salt and pepper to taste

Combine all ingredients and season to taste with salt and pepper.

# Green Tomatoes, Cherry Tomatoes & Tomatillos

## Fried Green Tomatoes with Roasted Red Bell Pepper Aioli

Serves 4 to 6

### Roasted Red Bell Pepper Aioli
2 red bell peppers, roasted
1 cup mayonnaise
Salt and pepper to taste

In a food processor, combine all ingredients.

### Fried Green Tomatoes
½ cup flour
½ cup cornmeal
½ cup panko breadcrumbs
Salt and pepper to taste
4 green tomatoes, sliced ¼-inch thick
3 egg whites, beaten
2 tablespoons butter
2 tablespoons grapeseed oil

In a medium bowl, combine flour, cornmeal and breadcrumbs, and season lightly with salt and pepper. Set aside.
Coat each tomato slice in egg white, then in breadcrumb mixture.
Heat butter and oil over medium high heat and fry tomato slices on both sides. Place on cooling rack to stay crisp. Serve with roasted red bell pepper aioli.

# Chili Verde

Serves 8 to 10

*This recipe was inspired by Margarita Carmona.*

2 cups olive oil

5 pounds pork butt, bone in,
  trimmed and cut into 1-inch cubes

2 heads garlic, chopped

Salt and pepper

½ large yellow onion, diced

## Salsa

3 pounds tomatillos, peeled and quartered

4 bell peppers, yellow, green and orange, sliced

1 fresh jalapeno, sliced (add more for a
  spicier salsa)

2 garlic cloves, diced

½ large yellow onion, sliced

## Garnish

1 bunch cilantro

3 limes, sliced

In a large stock pot, heat olive oil at medium-high, and add pork and 2 heads garlic. Season with salt and pepper. Bring to a boil; reduce heat and simmer 45 minutes; turn meat once or twice. Transfer pork and oil to a large bowl when well cooked on all sides.

Take ½ cup oil from cooked pork and place in stock pot; add diced onions and cook 10 minutes. Use a slotted spoon to transfer pork from bowl back to stock pot and continue cooking.

While pork and onions are cooking, mix together 2 cups water and all salsa ingredients. Place salsa mixture, in small batches, in food processor and pulse until combined and chunky.

Add the chunky salsa to pork, and simmer 90 minutes, until the pork is easily cut with a fork. Season to taste with salt and pepper.*

Divide among bowls and garnish with cilantro and lime slices. Serve with tortillas.

*At this point I like to cool the chili verde and refrigerate it a day or two. This lets the flavors meld together, and results in a more complex tasting chili verde.

Chili verde recipes call for pork butt, but other cuts work equally well. Chili verde is the ideal way to use all the packages of pork in your freezer that are without a home...shoulder chops, butt ends, whatever else is there. Trim off the fat and cut the meat into chunks. Remember to simmer the meat until it almost falls apart.

When stewing meats I always buy pieces and parts of grass-fed pork or beef or lamb with the bone in. Your butcher will be happy to sell you bone-in meat. Meat that's closest to the bone is sweet and full of flavor. You can add the larger bones to the stewing process. Don't forget to remove the bones before serving the stew.

# Green Tomatoes, Cherry Tomatoes & Tomatillos

ᶜ⟶ Try to think ahead when making any meal. For example, when I make chicken, I always save the back and neck bones. I keep them in a plastic bag in the freezer until I have enough to make soup stock.

## Green Tomato and Tarragon Chicken

Serves 6

Preheat oven to 350°F.

4 cups green tomatoes, small diced

1 tablespoon honey

½ cup water

2 tablespoons butter

2 tablespoons olive oil

2 chickens, cut into 8 pieces each

Salt and pepper to taste

1 cup cream

2 tablespoons fresh tarragon, chopped

3 tablespoons Parmesan cheese, shaved

In a small pot, cook tomatoes with honey and water 30 to 40 minutes. Purée until smooth. Mix in cream and tarragon. Set aside.

In a large sauté pan, heat butter and oil. Season chicken lightly with salt and pepper, and sear until golden brown. Transfer chicken to a large baking dish.

Pour tomato purée over chicken pieces.

Bake 45 to 60 minutes, until chicken is cooked through. Garnish with Parmesan cheese and tarragon.

# Spaghetti Sauce with Wild Meat

Serves 8 with plenty of leftovers

1 tablespoon olive oil

2 cups yellow onions, diced

4 cloves garlic, diced

½ cup bell pepper, diced

½ pound each ground elk, venison, grass fed
   pork and beef

2 cans organic diced tomatoes (28 ounces each)

1 bottle red wine (750 ml)

1½ tablespoons Italian seasoning

2 teaspoons salt

½ teaspoon pepper

½ pound mushrooms (crimini or oyster), sliced

½ cup celery leaves, finely sliced

Place olive oil in a large stainless steel pot and sauté onions, garlic and bell peppers until limp. Remove onion mixture from pot, and set aside. Sauté ground meats until slightly browned. Return onion mixture to pot and add tomatoes, wine, Italian seasoning, salt and pepper. Simmer on low heat 1½ hours. Add mushrooms and celery leaves, and simmer 20 minutes.

The sauce improves after sitting a day; it's even better on day three.

*Eat wild foods when you can.* –Michael Pollan

*Sculpture is the art of the hole and the lump.* —August Rodin

# September 24

# Peppers

Fried Padron Peppers

Pickle Relish

Steamed Mussels with Peppers and Crème Fraîche

Frittata with Broccoli and Peppers

Lamb Chops with Peppers

## Fried Padron Peppers

Serves 4

2 tablespoons grapeseed oil
1 pound Padron peppers
Salt and pepper to taste
½ teaspoon chili flakes (optional)

Heat oil in a large sauté pan. Fry peppers over medium heat until skins begin to blister. Remove from pan and season with salt, pepper and chili flakes. Serve warm.

Padron peppers are smaller, sweeter green bell peppers. Typically served as tapas in Spanish cuisine dishes, they are fast becoming a popular and healthy appetizer option on tables all across the country.

# Peppers

## Pickle Relish

Makes 6 pints

*Thanks to Brian Jansen for this recipe and for giving us a jar of relish.*

½ cup salt
8 cups Persian cucumbers, diced
4 cups green and red peppers, diced
2 cups onions, diced
1 tablespoon turmeric
½ cup brown sugar
4 cups vinegar
1 stick cinnamon
1 tablespoon mustard seed
⅛ teaspoon ground allspice
2 teaspoons whole cloves

In a large bowl combine salt and 8 cups water. Stir to dissolve salt. Add cucumbers, peppers, onions and turmeric. Cover and let stand 4 hours. Drain water and add 8 cups fresh cold water. Let stand 1 hour. Drain all liquid. Set aside.

In a large pot, mix together sugar and vinegar and bring to boil. While vinegar mixture is coming to a boil, place remaining spices in a piece of cheese cloth and add to pot. Once mixture is boiling, add vegetables. Turn off heat, cover and let stand 12 hours.

On day 2, bring vegetables to a boil. Reduce heat and simmer until hot throughout. Discard spice bag. Pack vegetables into clean jars, leaving ¼-inch headspace. Seal jars, and cook 10 minutes in water bath.

## Steamed Mussels with Peppers and Crème Fraîche

Serves 4

2½ pounds mussels
¾ cup crème fraîche
1 tablespoon lemon juice
4 teaspoons bell pepper (1 teaspoon each green, red, yellow and orange), finely diced
1½ teaspoons capers, chopped
½ teaspoon caper juice
2 teaspoons chives, sliced
Salt and pepper to taste

In a large pot, bring 3 quarts of water to a boil. Add mussels. Boil until mussels open. Immediately drain water. Set mussels aside. To make sauce, blend remaining ingredients. Divide mussels among 4 large bowls and drizzle sauce over top. Serve with a basket of sliced sourdough bread.

# Fritatta with Broccoli and Peppers

Serves 4

Preheat oven to 325°F.

10 eggs
¾ cup half and half
Salt and pepper to taste
1 tablespoon olive oil
1 tablespoon butter
½ cup onions, diced
1 clove garlic, minced
1½ cups broccoli, cut into florets
½ cup red bell peppers, diced
1 cup Gruyère cheese, grated

Whisk together eggs and half and half; season lightly with salt and pepper. Set aside.

In a 7-inch cast iron pan, heat oil and butter. Add onions and garlic and cook until fragrant. Add broccoli and peppers and continue to cook until just tender.

Turn heat to low, add egg mixture. Scrape bottom and sides of pan with a rubber spatula to prevent sticking.

Top with cheese, cover with foil and bake 20 to 25 minutes. Remove foil and continue baking until slightly firm to the touch. Slice and serve from the pan, or put on a platter.

# Lamb Chops with Peppers

Serves 4

8 lamb loin or rib chops
Salt and pepper to taste
1 tablespoon grapeseed oil
1 large yellow onion, julienne
2 cups peppers, mixed colors, julienne
1 cup celery leaves, sliced

Season lamb with salt and pepper. Heat oil in a large pan and sear lamb on both sides, about 2 minutes per side, depending on thickness. Remove from pan and cover to keep warm. Add additional oil to pan if needed. Place onion and pepper slices in pan and sauté until tender crisp. Add celery leaves and stir with sliced pepper mixture. Add salt and pepper if desired. Arrange lamb chops on serving platter, top with peppers. Serve with brown rice.

*Real dirt. Real food. Real health.*

# Apples

Autumn Quinoa

The World's Best Applesauce

Sautéed Apples

Autumn Apple Cake

Apple Galette

Apple Pie Full of Flavor

## No Farms, No Food

*Thanks to Christine Turner*

It takes 10,000 years to make an inch of top soil. Topsoil is the upper layer of soil where plants concentrate root growth. Topsoil sustains life on the planet. The American Farmland Trust uses this analogy to show how important topsoil is to life:

Imagine the Earth as an apple. If it were sliced into four pieces, three pieces represent the Earth's bodies of water. One piece represents the land.

If the remaining piece were sliced in half again, one piece represents land unsuitable or inhospitable for farming, e.g. deserts, mountains, ice and snow lands.

This leaves one-eighth (4/32) of the apple representing the land used to live on and grow food. Of that amount, 3/32 represents soils too poor to produce food or already covered by cities, roads and buildings. The remaining 1/32 of the apple is the portion of the Earth where food can grow. The peel represents the thin layer of topsoil that is used for food production.

AFT estimates "each year the United States alone loses over a million acres of farmland to conversion to non-agricultural uses, and we are losing the land most suited to grow food. More than 75% of America's fruits, vegetables and dairy products are produced on urban-edge farms and threatened by sprawling development."

The land sustains the farmers and ranchers who work hard to feed us. We need public policies that actively support and preserve the land. Clearly, everyone should care about what happens to land resources in their communities.

# Apples

## Autumn Quinoa

Serves 4 to 6

*Thanks to Patti Linn for this recipe.*

Preheat oven to 350°F.

2 cups butternut squash, peeled and diced
3 tablespoons olive oil
Salt and pepper to taste
1 cup quinoa
¼ cup dried cranberries
1 cup onions, diced
1 apple, diced
2 cloves garlic, minced
1 cup fresh apple juice
2 tablespoons pumpkin seeds, toasted

Toss squash with 2 tablespoons oil, salt and pepper. Spread on baking sheet and roast until tender, about 30 minutes.

While squash is roasting, cook quinoa following package directions, substituting chicken or vegetable broth for water. Remove from heat and add cranberries. Let sit 5 minutes. Fluff with fork and transfer to a large bowl.

Add remaining oil to a skillet, turn heat to medium. Add onions and cook a few minutes, until onions begin to soften. Add apples and garlic and cook, stirring for a few minutes. Add apple juice and continue cooking until liquid is reduced by half. Remove from heat and add to quinoa mixture. Stir in pumpkin seeds. Serve warm or at room temperature.

*Why do we need so many kinds of apples? Because there are so many folks. A person has a right to gratify his legitimate taste. If he wants 20 or 40 kinds of apples for his personal use he should be accorded the privilege. There is merit in variety itself. It provides more contact with life, and leads away from uniformity and monotony.*
*–Liberty Hyde Bailey*

## The World's Best Applesauce

Serves 6

4 pounds cooking apples, peeled and quartered (save peelings)
1 cup fresh unfiltered, unsweetened apple juice
½ lemon, peeled, peelings julienne
¼ cup lemon juice (from peeled lemon)
1 cinnamon stick, 4 inches long
⅓ cup brown sugar
2 tablespoons granulated sugar
½ teaspoon salt

Place apple peels in 2-quart sauce pan. Add ¼ to ⅓ cup apple juice. Cover and simmer 1 hour, or until peels can be easily pierced with a kitchen fork. (After 20 minutes check to make sure there is enough juice in the pan so peelings do not burn; add more juice if necessary.)

Remove pan from heat and cool slightly; purée apple peelings with a hand blender. Set aside.

Place quartered apples, lemon peel, lemon juice, cinnamon, sugars, salt and remaining apple juice in a large sauce pan or pot. Bring to a boil, reduce heat, and simmer until apples are falling apart. Remove from heat; remove cinnamon stick and lemon peelings. Mash apples roughly with a potato masher. Gently fold puréed apple peelings into apples until well blended.

To serve: Place ½ cup apple sauce in small bowls; top with a teaspoon of crème fraîche or a sprinkle of crystallized ginger chips.

# Sautéed Apples

Serves 4 to 6

2 tablespoons butter
4 cooking apples, peeled and sliced
3 tablespoons brown sugar
½ teaspoon ground cinnamon
⅛ teaspoon ground nutmeg
Vanilla yogurt, crème fraîche or ice cream

In a skillet, heat butter until bubbly. Add sliced apples and sauté 4 to 5 minutes. Add brown sugar and spices. Cook 2 to 3 minutes. (For added flavor, stir in a tablespoon of Triple Sec with the brown sugar.)
Spoon apples into small dessert bowls. Top with a dollop of vanilla yogurt, crème fraîche or ice cream.
Use this recipe for sautéed blackberries, sliced strawberries or sliced peaches. Be careful not to overcook.

# Autumn Apple Cake

Serves 6

*Thanks to Susan Dupre for this recipe.*

Preheat oven to 350°F.

1 cup sifted flour
1 teaspoon baking powder
½ teaspoon cinnamon
½ teaspoon nutmeg
½ teaspoon salt
3 tablespoons butter
1 cup sugar
1 egg, beaten
3 cups apples, peeled and diced
1 teaspoon vanilla
½ cup chopped walnuts or pecans

Sift flour, baking powder, spices and salt together. Set aside.
Cream butter and sugar, add egg and mix together. Add flour mix to creamed mixture. Stir in diced apples, vanilla and nuts.
Pour into greased 8x8-inch pan. Bake 50 minutes.

# Apples

## Apple Galette

Serves 6 to 8

Preheat oven to 400°F.

### Galette dough for 9-inch pie

3 tablespoons vegetable shortening
3 tablespoons butter
1 cup all purpose flour
2 tablespoons cold water
1 teaspoon cinnamon
1 teaspoon sugar (mix with cinnamon)
½ teaspoon Demerara sugar (optional)

Use a pie dough cutter to blend shortening, butter, flour and salt to cornmeal stage. Slowly add cold water, mixing with a fork until dough comes together. Add more water if necessary. Form into a ball, cover and chill at least 2 hours before rolling out.
In the palm of your hand, form ball into round flat disk. Roll dough on a floured surface until it is ⅛-inch thick. Dough will be 14 to16 inches in diameter. Place in bottom of 9-inch pie pan; dough will fall over edges of pan.

### Filling

½ cup sugar
3 tablespoons all purpose flour
1 teaspoon cinnamon
½ teaspoon salt
4½ cups Gravenstein apples, sliced
2 teaspoons cold butter

Blend sugar, flour, cinnamon and salt. Set aside. Layer half the apples in the center of the galette shell. Sprinkle half the sugar mixture over apples. Repeat using remaining apples and sugar. Distribute small butter pieces evenly over fruit. Bring edges of dough toward the center over the fruit and staple to fruit with toothpicks. There will be a small opening in the middle. Sprinkle top of crust with cinnamon sugar, then Demerara.
Bake until a toothpick inserted comes out clean and juices are bubbling around the crust, 45 to 50 minutes.

*Good apple pies are a considerable part of our domestic happiness.*
*—Jane Austen*

*If you want to make an apple pie from scratch, you must first create the universe. –Carl Sagan*

# Apple Pie Full of Flavor

Serves 8

Preheat oven to 400°F.

## Two crust pie dough for 9-inch pie

¼ cup vegetable shortening

¼ cup cold butter

1½ cups all purpose flour

½ teaspoon salt

¼ cup cold water

½ teaspoon cinnamon

½ teaspoon sugar (mix with cinnamon)

1 teaspoon Demerara sugar (optional)


Use a pie dough cutter to blend shortening, butter, flour and salt to cornmeal stage. Slowly add cold water, mixing with a fork until dough comes together. Add more water if necessary. Form into a ball, cover and chill at least 2 hours before rolling out.

Cut the dough ball into two pieces, one slightly larger than the other. Roll out the dough on a floured surface until ⅛-inch thick. Make dough 10 inches for bottom, and 9 inches for top. Place filling in the shell. Apply top crust. Trim, roll and crimp edges. Score the dough 6 or 7 places to allow air to vent. Sprinkle top with cinnamon sugar mixture, then Demerara.

## Filling

5 cups apples, peeled and sliced (save peelings)

⅓ cup fresh apple juice

⅔ cup sugar

1 teaspoon cinnamon

2 tablespoons flour

½ teaspoon salt

1 tablespoon cold butter


Place apple peels in 2-quart sauce pan. Add ¼ to ⅓ cup apple juice. Cover and simmer 1 hour or until peels can be easily pierced with a kitchen fork. After 20 minutes check to make there is enough juice in the pan so peelings do not burn; add more juice if necessary.

Remove pan from heat and cool slightly; purée the peelings with a hand blender. Set aside. Blend sugar, cinnamon, flour and salt. Set aside. Place the sliced apples in a large bowl. Add the peeling purée and toss apples until purée is distributed over apples. Place half the apples in pie pan and top with half of the sugar mixture. Cover with remaining apples and top with remaining sugar mixture. Distribute small pieces of butter over apples.

Bake 50 to 60 minutes. Cool before slicing and serving.

*October 8*

# Persimmons

Persimmon Dip

Persimmon Chutney

Grilled Fuyu Persimmon Salad with Balsamic Vinaigrette

Cranberry Sauce

Spice Rubbed Brisket with Persimmon Glaze

Persimmon Loaf

Visitors to our home know which fruits and vegetables are in season because they're right there on the dining room table or the kitchen counter. Every week I carefully arrange an attractive centerpiece or counter display using in-season produce. It gives the kitchen and dining room a festive air and lots of color.

Local artist Anthony Maki Gill made several narrow platters with simple legs to display produce down the middle of our long walnut table. His smaller dishes are just right for petite spaces or to display a vignette of produce. If guests or visitors comment on the produce arrangement, I immediately place it in a reusable or recyclable bag, usually brown paper, and send it home with them. It's our way of spreading the joy of eating food that's fresh, local and in season. Once people taste the difference in texture and taste, they're hooked. And it's not surprising to see them at next week's farmers market or at the nursery purchasing plants for their gardens.

# Persimmons

## Persimmon Dip

Makes 6 cups

*Thanks to Lori Boone for this recipe.*

6 to 8 Fuyu persimmons, diced into small cubes
2 to 3 ripe avocados, diced into small cubes
2 limes, juiced
2 bell peppers, one red and one green, diced
2 large tomatoes, diced
1 bunch cilantro, stems removed, leaves chopped
6 green onions, sliced
2 small yellow onions, diced
4 Serrano peppers, finely diced
Salt and pepper

Place persimmons, avocados, lime juice, bell
peppers, tomatoes, cilantro, green onions and
yellow onions in large bowl. Add Serrano
peppers, salt and pepper to taste. Mix well.
Refrigerate 12 hours.

## Persimmon Chutney

Makes 3 cups

2 cups Hachiya persimmon pulp, puréed
1 cup Fuyu persimmon, peeled and small diced
½ cup pomegranate seeds
2 tablespoons crystallized ginger, minced

Combine above ingredients. Great with fish or
chicken.

*Shop the peripheries of the supermarket and
stay out of the middle.     –Michael Pollan*

# Grilled Fuyu Persimmon Salad with Balsamic Vinaigrette

Serves 4

Preheat grill.

6 Fuyu persimmons, peeled and sliced ½–inch thick
1 tablespoon olive oil
½ pomegranate seeds
½ cup almonds, toasted

## Balsamic Vinaigrette

2 tablespoons balsamic vinegar
1 tablespoon olive oil
2 tablespoons honey
Salt and pepper to taste

Brush persimmon slices with oil and place them on hot, clean grill. Grill 1 minute each side, until grill marks persimmons. Remove and cool on a baking sheet.
When cool, place in a large bowl, and add pomegranate seeds and almonds.
Combine vinaigrette ingredients and toss with salad.

Hoshigaki are persimmons that have been dried over a period of several weeks. They are hung and then hand massaged several times a day until the sugars inside the fruit produce a frost-like dusting on the outside. The fruit is tender and moist, and the flavor concentrated. It is almost a lost art.

# Persimmons

## Cranberry Sauce

Makes 6 cups

*Thanks to Ivette Rothenberg for this recipe.*

2 packages fresh cranberries
1 cup mandarin juice
1 teaspoon mandarin zest
1 cup water
1½ cups sugar
1 cup mandarins, segmented and sliced into
　　½-inch pieces
1 cup Fuyu persimmons, sliced into ½-inch pieces
¼ teaspoon nutmeg

Place cranberries, mandarin juice, zest, water and sugar in a large sauce pan; bring to a boil.
Reduce heat and simmer until cranberries pop open. Add mandarins, persimmons, and nutmeg. Stir until combined.
Remove from heat and cool.
Serve chilled or at room temperature.

## Spice Rubbed Brisket with Persimmon Glaze

Serves 8

Preheat oven to 325°F.

1 beef brisket, 2 to 3 pounds
1 tablespoon dried sage
1 tablespoon dried thyme
2 teaspoons brown sugar
Salt and pepper to taste
2 cups beef stock
1 cup Fuyu persimmon, peeled and julienne
½ cup green cabbage, julienne
½ cup red cabbage, julienne
8 small French rolls

Generously rub brisket on all sides with spices, brown sugar, salt and pepper. Place in roasting pan with stock and cook 3 to 4 hours, until tender.
When done cooking, shred beef, toss with persimmon glaze, and keep warm until time to serve.
In a large bowl, toss Fuyu persimmon with cabbages, and season to taste with salt and pepper.
To assemble, place brisket and cabbage mixture on each roll and serve.

### Persimmon Glaze

1 cup Hachiya persimmon pulp, puréed
1 tablespoon molasses
1 lemon, juiced
Salt and pepper to taste

Combine glaze ingredients in a small saucepan and simmer 2 to 3 minutes.

# Persimmon Loaf

Serves 12

*Thanks to Dot Hummert for this recipe.*

Preheat oven to 300°F.

1 lemon, juice and zest
½ cup raisins
¾ cup sugar
½ cup butter
1 egg
1 cup Hachiya persimmon pulp, puréed
2 teaspoons baking soda
1½ cups flour
½ teaspoon ground cloves
½ teaspoon allspice
1 teaspoon cinnamon
½ cup walnuts, chopped

Pour lemon juice over raisins and let sit several hours. This allows the raisins to plump.
In a separate bowl, cream sugar and butter until mixture is fluffy. Add egg and beat.
Mix puréed pulp with baking soda, and add to butter mixture. Blend flour and spices into mixture. Fold in nuts, lemon zest and raisins.
Pour into two 4x8-inch well-buttered loaf pans. Bake 45 to 50 minutes. Cool 10 minutes and invert onto a wire rack.

For the persimmon loaf, use fully ripened Hachiya persimmons. This means waiting until they are gelatinous to the touch. Cut off the stem and gently slice persimmon in half vertically. Remove the seeds. Use a hand blender to purée the persimmon meat and skin.

Soft Fuju persimmons can be used instead, but the Hachiya has a more complex flavor. To soften a persimmon, place it in the freezer for a day. The persimmon will be soft enough to purée but not as flavorful as a fully ripe one.

*October 15*

# Eggplant

Baba Ganoush

Greek–Style Quinoa Salad

Grilled Eggplant Sandwich with Sun–Dried Tomato Aioli

Pork Ribs with Mustard Barbecue Sauce

# Eggplant

In French, chiffonade means "made of rags." In the kitchen, it means to cut vegetables, usually lettuces or herbs, into thin strips or shreds.

## Baba Ganoush

Serves 6

Preheat oven to 400°F.

2 medium eggplants
2 tablespoons lemon juice
2 cloves garlic, chopped
2 tablespoons olive oil
2 tablespoons parsley, chopped
Salt and pepper to taste
Parsley for garnish
12 slices rustic bread, grilled

Puncture eggplant with a fork, place on a baking sheet, cover with foil, and roast 30 to 45 minutes, until soft. Turn halfway through. Cool slightly.

Cut eggplant in half and scoop flesh into a food processor. Add lemon and garlic and process until smooth. Slowly add oil and continue to process. Add salt and pepper to taste.

Garnish with parsley and serve with grilled bread.

## Greek-Style Quinoa Salad

Serves 6

2 cups quinoa
1 tablespoon grapeseed oil
1 large eggplant, small diced
1 cup Persian or English cucumbers, small diced
½ cup olives, halved
1 pint cherry tomatoes, halved
¼ cup basil, chiffonade
2 tablespoons parsley, chopped
¼ cup red wine vinegar
½ cup olive oil
2 lemons, juiced
Salt and pepper to taste

Cook quinoa in 3½ cups salted water until tender, about 20 to 25 minutes. Drain and transfer to a large bowl. Cool.
Heat grapeseed oil in sauté pan. Add eggplant and sauté until caramelized. Add to quinoa.
Add remaining ingredients and season to taste with salt and pepper.

# Eggplant

## Grilled Eggplant Sandwich with Sun-Dried Tomato Aioli

Serves 4

Preheat grill.

### Sun-Dried Tomato Aioli
2 egg yolks
½ lemon, juiced
1 to 1½ cups olive oil
¼ cup sun-dried tomatoes, minced
Salt and pepper to taste

Whisk together egg yolks and lemon juice. Slowly add oil while whisking. If aioli gets too thick, add a few drops of water. When fully emulsified, stir in tomatoes, and season to taste with salt and pepper. Aioli keeps in refrigerator up to a week.

### Grilled Eggplant Sandwich
2 medium eggplants, sliced ¾-inch thick
2 tablespoons olive oil
Salt and pepper to taste
4 ciabatta rolls, cut in half
3 ounces feta cheese, crumbled
2 cups arugula leaves

Season eggplant with olive oil, salt and pepper, and place on hot, clean grill. Grill 1 minute each side, until grill marks eggplant. Remove and set aside.
Place rolls on the grill until toasted. Remove. To serve, spread aioli on both sides of rolls. Place eggplant slices, feta cheese and arugula on bottom, and top with other half. Slice in half and serve.

# Pork Ribs with Mustard Barbecue Sauce

Serves 6

Preheat oven to 300°F.

3 racks six-bone pork ribs

Salt and pepper to taste

1 tablespoon grapeseed oil

1½ cups onion, diced

3 cloves garlic, minced

2 cups apple cider vinegar

2 teaspoons chili flakes

1 bay leaf

1 tablespoon thyme, chopped

1½ cups brown sugar

½ cup Seeds and Suds Mendocino Mustard (or a good dark mustard)

¾ cup yellow mustard

Season ribs with salt and pepper. Cover and roast 2 hours.

To make barbecue sauce, heat oil in a medium saucepan, and cook onions and garlic until fragrant. Add vinegar, spices and sugar. Bring to a boil. Reduce heat and simmer 45 minutes. Remove from heat, stir in mustards and season to taste with salt and pepper.

Coat ribs with barbecue sauce. Return to oven and bake 1 hour, until meat is tender. Finish under broiler if desired.

*www.theartofrealfood.com*

# Pears

Pear Salad with Apple Juice Vinaigrette

Quinoa with Pears

Figs with Asian Pears and Yogurt

Pear Sauce with Ginger Chips

Pear Crumble

Brownies

Asian Pear Pie

Asian Pear Cake

## Pear Salad with Apple Juice Vinaigrette

Serves 4

3 cups spinach leaves
2 pears, sliced
1 ounce gouda cheese, shaved
¼ cup pecans, toasted

### Apple Juice Vinaigrette

2 cups apple juice or cider, reduced to ½ cup
2 tablespoons apple cider vinegar
¼ cup olive oil
Salt and pepper to taste

Combine vinaigrette ingredients and season to taste with salt and pepper. Toss with salad ingredients and serve immediately.

# Pears

## Quinoa with Pears

Serves 6

2 cups quinoa
⅔ cup apple cider vinegar
⅔ cup olive oil
2 Asian pears, diced
½ cup pomegranate seeds
½ cup pecans, toasted
Salt and pepper to taste
2 ounces Shaft blue cheese, crumbled

Cook quinoa in 3½ cups salted water until tender,
about 20 to 25 minutes. Drain and transfer to a
large mixing bowl; cool.
Combine with vinegar, oil, pears, pomegranate
seeds and pecans. Season to taste with salt and
pepper and garnish with blue cheese.

# Figs with Asian Pears and Yogurt

Serves 4

8 figs, halved
3 ripe Asian pears, cut into wedges
1½ cups Greek yogurt
2 tablespoons mint, chiffonade

In 4 small bowls, arrange figs and pears, top with yogurt and garnish with mint.

# Pear Sauce with Ginger Chips

Serves 4 to 6

2 pounds Bosc pears, peeled, sliced into 1-inch pieces
¼ cup pear or apple juice
¼ cup crystallized ginger pieces

Place pear slices in 2-quart sauce pan, add juice, and simmer until soft. Mash with a potato masher. Fold in ginger pieces.
Serve warm or chilled.

We use crystallized ginger pieces from The Ginger People. Look in the baking section at the local grocery store, or online at www.thegingerpeople.com.

# Pears

## Pear Crumble

Serves 8

Preheat oven to 375°F.

8 pears (firm, just beginning to turn yellow),
   peeled and sliced (save peelings)
¼ cup pear or apple juice
½ cup sugar
⅓ cup tapioca flour
¼ teaspoon ground ginger
Dash nutmeg
1 tablespoon lemon juice
½ cup chopped walnuts or pecans

Place peelings in a 2-quart sauce pan. Add juice.
Cover, and simmer 45 minutes or until peels are
easily pierced with a kitchen fork. After 20
minutes check to make sure there is enough juice
in the pan so peelings don't burn; add more juice
if necessary.

Remove pan from heat and cool slightly; purée
peelings with a hand blender. Set aside.

In a large bowl, mix together sliced pears, sugar,
tapioca flour, ginger and nutmeg. Add peeling
purée and toss lightly.

Sprinkle with lemon juice. Let sit 20 minutes. Stir
and place in buttered 9x13-inch baking dish.
Gently press nuts onto pears and cover with
crumb topping.

Bake 45 to 50 minutes.

### Crumb Topping

6 tablespoons butter
⅔ cup brown sugar
⅔ cup flour
½ teaspoon cinnamon

Mix butter, brown sugar, flour, and cinnamon
together for crumb topping.

# Brownies

Makes 2 dozen

Preheat oven to 350°F.

*This recipe adapted from the 1963 edition "Joy
of Cooking."*

¾ cup butter
4 ounces unsweetened organic chocolate
4 eggs, room temperature
½ teaspoon salt
2 cups sugar
1 teaspoon vanilla
1 cup all purpose flour, sifted
1 cup pecans, diced

Melt butter and chocolate in a double boiler. Set
aside to cool. (If you don't, your brownies will be
heavy and dry.)

Beat eggs and salt until light and foamy. Add
sugar and vanilla gradually, and continue beating
until well creamed. Set aside.

With a few swift strokes, stir cooled chocolate
mixture into eggs and sugar.

Before mixture becomes uniformly colored, fold
in flour. Before flour is uniformly colored, gently
stir in pecans.

Bake in a 9x13-inch pan about 25 minutes. Cut
when cool.

Garnish with whipped cream.

# Asian Pear Pie

Serves 8

Preheat oven to 400°F.

## Two crust pie dough for 9-inch pie

¼ cup vegetable shortening

¼ cup cold butter

1½ cups all purpose flour

½ teaspoon salt

¼ cup cold water

½ teaspoon cinnamon

½ teaspoon sugar (mix with cinnamon)

1 teaspoon Demerara sugar (optional)

Use a pie dough cutter to blend shortening, butter, flour and salt to cornmeal stage. Slowly add cold water, mixing with a fork until dough comes together. Add more water if necessary. Form into a ball, cover and chill at least 2 hours before rolling out.

Cut the dough ball into two pieces, one slightly larger than the other. Roll out the dough on a floured surface until ⅛-inch thick. Make dough 10 inches for bottom, and 9 inches for top. Place filling in the shell. Apply top crust. Trim, roll and crimp edges. Score the dough 6 or 7 places to allow air to vent. Sprinkle top with cinnamon sugar mixture, then Demerara.

## Filling

⅓ cup sugar

⅓ cup brown sugar

⅓ cup tapioca flour

½ teaspoon salt

1 teaspoon cinnamon

½ teaspoon almond extract

½ teaspoon vanilla extract

5 cups mixed Asian pears, peeled and sliced

1 tablespoon butter

In a large bowl, blend sugars, tapioca flour, salt, cinnamon, almond and vanilla extracts. Set aside. Layer half of the pears in the pie shell and sprinkle half the sugar mixture over pears. Repeat using remaining pears and sugar. Distribute small pieces of butter evenly over fruit. Bake pie until a toothpick inserted comes out clean and juices are bubbling around the crust, 50 to 60 minutes.

# Asian Pear Cake

Serves 8

*Thanks to Candee Kenny for this recipe.*

Preheat oven to 350°F.

2 cups flour

1 teaspoon salt

2 teaspoons cinnamon or 1 teaspoon
   4% cinnamon

1 teaspoon nutmeg

2 teaspoons baking soda

2 cups sugar

½ cup vegetable oil

2 eggs

4 cups Asian pears, diced

Sift together flour, salt, spices and baking soda. Set aside.

In a mixing bowl, combine sugar, oil and eggs until well incorporated. Stir in pears. Add dry ingredients and mix to combine.

Pour into greased 9x13-inch pan and bake 1 hour. If desired, top with powdered sugar or whipped cream. Unfrosted, this cake makes a great breakfast.

# Winter Squash

Butternut Squash Salad with Goat Cheese Vinaigrette
Grilled Candy Squash
Butternut Squash and Mushroom Casserole
Roasted Delicata Squash with Apples and Walnuts
Roasted Hubbard and Marina d'Chioggia Squash
Pumpkin (or Squash) Pie
Heirloom Pumpkin Pie with Walnut Crust

The cookware in my cupboards has lived there more than 40 years. Originally many of the cast iron skillets and Pyrex dishes were in my mother's cupboard. That makes some of them 60 or 70 years old.

I prefer cast iron skillets for frying or sautéing,

and the pans are an ideal way to present a rustic meal. The skillets cook evenly and hold the heat longer. Rub them with a light coat of vegetable oil after each use to keep them looking new. How much oil?

Enough to restore the sheen. Well-seasoned cast iron pans last a hundred years.

Pyrex dishes and pans are best for casseroles, soufflés, or pastries. Glass dishes bake evenly, and I appreciate being able to see when the food is nicely browned.

For sautéing, steaming, or pan cooking with water, I use seven-ply stainless steel cookware. Many years ago I had the good sense to invest in quality cookware; it was the right thing to do. If I think about the cost, it ends up being a very good choice – the cost of my cookware amortized over many years amounts to less than $8 a year. Investing in good cookware is a good idea.

# Winter Squash

## Butternut Squash Salad with Goat Cheese Vinaigrette

*Thanks to Debbie Dutra for this recipe.*

Serves 4

1 medium butternut squash, peeled and julienne
½ cup dried cherries
½ cup walnuts, toasted
¼ cup parsley, chopped

### Goat Cheese Vinaigrette

4 ounces goat cheese, room temperature
2 tablespoons honey
3 tablespoons olive oil
2 teaspoons apple cider vinegar
½ Meyer lemon, juiced
Salt and pepper to taste

Combine vinaigrette ingredients. Add salt and pepper to taste.

Toss squash, cherries and walnuts with vinaigrette. Make at least 1 hour ahead to allow flavors to combine. Garnish with parsley before serving.

## Grilled Candy Squash

Serves 6 to 8

Preheat grill.

1 candy squash, 2 to 3 pounds
2 tablespoons olive oil
Salt and pepper to taste

Cut squash into ¾-inch slices and remove seeds. Brush both sides with oil and season with salt and pepper. Grill until marked on both sides and knife tender, about 4 to 5 minutes per side.

# Butternut Squash and Mushroom Casserole

Serves 8

*Thanks to Debbie Dutra for this recipe.*

Preheat oven to 375°F.

4 cups butternut squash, sliced into
  ¾-inch squares

1 tablespoon olive oil

2 leeks, tops removed, washed, green and
  white part thinly sliced

2 to 3 cloves garlic

¼ cup butter

1 pound crimini mushrooms,
  quartered bite size pieces

2 tablespoons fresh thyme leaves, chopped

Salt and pepper to taste

6 cups cubed artisan bread, 1-inch pieces

2 tablespoons flour

3½ cups half and half

5 large eggs

⅓ cup Parmesan cheese, grated

1½ cups Gruyère cheese, grated

Toss squash with olive oil until well coated. Place squash on sheet tray lined with parchment paper,

and roast 30 to 35 minutes, until tender. Toss squash after 15 minutes so it cooks evenly.

While squash is cooking, sauté leeks and garlic in 1 tablespoon butter until brown. Remove to a large bowl. Using same pan, add 1 tablespoon butter and sauté mushrooms until brown; add thyme. Add mushrooms and roasted squash to leeks. Salt and pepper to taste.

Briefly toast bread cubes in oven and add to squash mixture. Mix well. Place bread and squash mixture into a well-buttered casserole dish or 13x9-inch pan. Set aside.

In a sauté pan melt remaining butter; add flour and cook over medium heat 2 to 3 minutes. Whisk in 1½ cups half and half and just bring to a boil. In a separate bowl, whisk remaining half and half with eggs and Parmesan cheese. Slowly add heated half and half; stir to combine. Pour over squash mixture and sprinkle top with Gruyère cheese.

Bake uncovered 30 minutes, until the cheese is melted and slightly browned.

You can make this dish a day ahead, and instead of baking it, cover it and put it in the refrigerator overnight to let the flavors meld. Bring pan to room temperature before baking.

# Winter Squash

## Roasted Delicata Squash with Apples and Walnuts

Serves 6

Preheat oven to 350°F.

3 delicata squashes, halved lengthwise,
  seeds removed
1 tablespoon olive oil
Salt and pepper to taste
¼ cup butter
3 apples, peeled and diced
¼ cup brown sugar
2 teaspoons rosemary, chopped
½ cup walnuts
1 teaspoon nutmeg

Coat squash with olive oil, salt and pepper.
Roast, cut side down, 25 minutes, until fork
tender.
Meanwhile, heat butter in a large sauté pan and
add apples. Cook over high heat, until apples
begin to caramelize. Add brown sugar and
rosemary and continue to cook until sugar melts.
Pile apples into roasted squash, top with walnuts
and sprinkle with nutmeg. Return to oven and
bake 15 minutes.

## Roasted Hubbard and Marina d'Chioggia Squash

Serves 4

Preheat oven to 375°F.

3 cups Hubbard squash, peeled and cut into
  1-inch pieces
3 cups Marina d'Chioggia squash, peeled and
  cut into 1-inch pieces
2 tablespoons olive oil
Salt and pepper to taste

Toss Hubbard squash with 1 tablespoon oil, salt
and pepper. Transfer to roasting tray. Repeat for
Marina d'Chioggia. Roast on separate sheet trays,
30 to 40 minutes, until knife tender. Toss
together and season to taste with salt and
pepper. Garnish with your favorite herb.

# Pumpkin (or Squash) Pie

Serves 8

1½ cups cooked pumpkin or squash

1½ cups evaporated milk or rich cream

6 tablespoons brown sugar

2 tablespoons white sugar

½ teaspoon salt

1 teaspoon cinnamon

½ teaspoon ginger

¼ teaspoon cloves

½ cup dark corn syrup or light molasses

3 eggs, slightly beaten

1 teaspoon vanilla or 2 tablespoons brandy or rum

1 cup heavy cream, whipped with 1 teaspoon sugar

Mix pumpkin, evaporated milk, sugars, salt, spices, corn syrup, and eggs in top of double boiler and cook over water until thick. Cool slightly and add vanilla.

Pour mixture into 9-inch baked pie shell. Chill until set.

Serve with a dollop of whipped cream.

# Heirloom Pumpkin Pie with Walnut Crust

Serves 8 to 10

Preheat oven to 325°F.

## Single crust for 9-inch pie

¾ cup walnuts, finely diced

¾ cup graham cracker crumbs

½ cup brown sugar, finely packed

1 teaspoon mandarin zest

¾ teaspoon cinnamon

½ teaspoon ground ginger

½ teaspoon salt

¼ cup butter, melted

> ❧ How do you know when your pumpkin pie is done? Insert a knife about an inch from the center of the pie. If the knife comes out clean, the pie is done. Tiny bubbles around the edge of the pie or filling that has separated from the crust are signs the pie is over-done, and you should remove it from the oven immediately.

Combine walnuts, graham cracker crumbs, brown sugar, zest cinnamon, ginger and salt. Pour melted butter over mixture and thoroughly mix with a fork. Press evenly into a 9-inch pie plate. Bake until lightly browned, 10 to 12 minutes

## Filling

Preheat oven to 300°F.

1 Winter Luxury pumpkin, 4 to 5 pounds, seeds removed, cleaned, cut into chunks

10 ounces Gina Marie Cream Cheese, room temperature

¾ cup sugar

1 teaspoon cinnamon

1 teaspoon ground ginger

1 teaspoon ground nutmeg

½ teaspoon salt

2 teaspoons vanilla

2 large eggs, room temperature

1 cup heavy cream, whipped (optional)

Place pumpkin chunks in a large steamer basket, cover and steam until tender. Cool.

Remove pulp from skins, and place 2½ cups of pulp in a bowl; purée with hand mixer. Set aside. In a separate bowl, use hand mixer to cream cheese, sugar, spices and salt until light and smooth. Add vanilla and eggs. Add pumpkin pulp and blend thoroughly.

Place in baked crust and bake 30 to 35 minutes, until the pie center has just set. Cool.

Top each slice with a dollop of whipped cream.

*November 5*

# Celery

Bloody Mary with Celery

Heirloom Cannellini Bean, Ham and Celery Soup

Scotch Broth

Salmon with Celery Root Purée

I've been shopping at farmers markets more than 30 years. You might think I've seen it all, but every season I find something new to get excited about. This fall Laura and I discovered dark green celery, so dark it makes grocery store celery look anemic. We bought some, of course, and found the flavor wonderfully hearty. Since this celery wasn't packaged for shipping, it still had a full head of leaves, which we chopped and used in stir fries. I've since learned most commercial growers produce blanched celery, which means they intentionally keep celery light in color. The result is a milder flavor, closer to that of celery heart. Unfortunately, the lighter color also means lower vitamin content.

With only six calories per eight-inch stalk, celery is definitely a low-calorie snack. It adds a crunch to salads, and texture to soups and stews.

I also like to use celery in side dishes and in juices. High in dietary fiber and loaded with vitamins and minerals, celery reduces blood pressure, improves the immune system, and promotes cardiovascular and joint health.

# Celery

## Bloody Mary with Celery

Makes 1 drink

Gary Romano's Organic Bloody Mary Mix
Dash Worcestershire sauce
Sprinkling salt
1 stalk dark green celery

Fill a tall glass with ice and pour in Bloody Mary mix. Add a dash of Worcestershire and a sprinkling of salt. Finish the drink off with a stalk of celery and you have a refreshing and tasty glass of good health.
If you prefer, add 1 ounce vodka with the drink mix.

## Heirloom Cannellini Bean, Ham and Celery Soup

Serves 4

¾ cup dried heirloom cannellini beans
1 ham bone or small piece of ham
6 cups water
3 bay leaves
6 black peppercorns
6 whole cloves
1 cup carrots, diced
3 celery ribs with leaves, chopped
1 cup yellow onions, diced
2 cloves garlic, minced
Salt and pepper to taste
1 cup Savoy cabbage, thinly sliced

Cover beans with water and soak overnight. Drain and place beans in large soup pot.
Add ham bone, water; wrap bay leaves, peppercorns and cloves in cheesecloth and add. Bring to a boil, reduce heat, and simmer until beans are soft, about 2½ to 3 hours.
During last 30 minutes add carrots, celery, onions and garlic. Remove ham from pot, mince, and add to soup; discard cheesecloth with herbs. Add salt and pepper to taste. Serve soup topped with Savoy cabbage.

# Scotch Broth

*Thanks to Dan Macon for this recipe.*

Serves 6 to 8

## Broth

3 pounds lamb shoulder chops

8 cups water

1 teaspoon salt

2 stalks celery, cut into 4-inch pieces

2 carrots, cut into quarters

1 onion, quartered

Make broth a day ahead: Place lamb, water, salt, celery, carrots and onions in a large sauce pan and cook 1 to 1½ hours, until the lamb is tender. Discard vegetables. Take lamb out of broth and remove meat from bones. Set aside.
Let broth cool; skim off fat. Return meat to broth.

½ cup barley

2 tablespoons butter

2 carrots, diced

2 stalks celery, diced

2 small white turnips or rutabagas,
  peeled and diced

1 medium yellow onion, diced

Salt and pepper to taste

Place barley in 4 cups water and cook 25 to 35 minutes, until tender. Drain and set aside.
Melt the butter in a skillet. Add carrots, celery, turnips and onion; sauté over low heat 7 to 10 minutes.
Heat broth. Add vegetables and cooked barley. Salt and pepper to taste.

*Eat mostly plants, especially leaves.*
*—Michael Pollan*

# Salmon with Celery Root Purée

Serves 6 to 8

1 tablespoon butter

4 cups celery root, peeled and large diced

1 cup cream

Salt and pepper to taste

2 tablespoons grapeseed oil

2 pounds salmon filets

¼ cup celery leaves

Heat butter in a medium pot. Add celery root and cream and season lightly with salt and pepper. Bring to a boil. Reduce heat and gently simmer until tender.
Place in food processor or blender and purée until smooth. Check seasoning and set aside.
In a large sauté pan, heat oil. Season fish with salt and pepper and sear on both sides. Remove from pan and serve on bed of celery root purée. Garnish with celery leaves.

When recipes call for celery root instead of celery, you might scratch your head and wonder what the chef is talking about. Celery root and celery are two distinct vegetables from the same family. Celery root, also called celeriac, is a root vegetable that grows like a carrot or turnip. It looks like a brown, knobby softball with little roots sticking out. Although it is somewhat of an ugly duckling in the vegetable world, celeriac has many of the same health benefits as celery with a more delicate flavor. It also has calming and pain relieving properties.

# Honey

St. Nick Melon with Honey and Walnuts

Buttermilk Biscuits with Honey Butter

Carrot Cookie Sandwiches with Honey Frosting

Many people believe all sugars are equal and that it doesn't matter whether you use honey, molasses, maple syrup, agave nectar, white or brown sugar in a recipe. There are basic differences in vitamin and mineral content and big differences in flavor and sweetness when you compare them all.

Honey and agave nectar are both sweeter than white sugar. Molasses has significantly higher vitamin content, and molasses and maple syrup both have a higher mineral content.

But let's talk flavor. A combination of honey and molasses adds a new dimension to the meaning of sweet, and 100% maple syrup is a familiar flavor in puddings, custards and baked goods.

Honey, however, remains my sweetener of choice. Local beekeepers do a nice job of placing hives in a variety of settings, which results in many distinctive flavors: orange, mandarin, apple, wildflower, clover and avocado. These honeys are available at farmers markets.

## St. Nick Melon with Honey and Walnuts

Serves 6

1 St. Nick melon, peeled, seeded and sliced
3 tablespoons honey
¼ cup walnuts, toasted
Salt and pepper to taste
Mint leaves, chiffonade

Combine melon, honey and walnuts, and season lightly with salt and pepper. Garnish with mint.

# Honey

## Buttermilk Biscuits with Honey Butter

Serves 6

Preheat oven to 450°F.

2 cups unbleached all purpose flour, plus more for dusting
¼ teaspoon baking soda
1 tablespoon baking powder (without aluminum)
1 teaspoon kosher salt or 1 teaspoon salt
6 tablespoons unsalted butter, very cold
1 cup buttermilk

Combine dry ingredients. Cut butter into chunks and cut into flour until it resembles coarse meal. If using a food processor, just pulse a few times until this consistency is achieved.

Add buttermilk and mix just until combined. Mix should be quite wet. Add more buttermilk gradually if mix seems too dry.

Turn dough out onto a floured board. Gently pat (do not roll) dough out until it's about ½–inch thick. Fold dough about 5 times, gently pressing it down until it is about 1 inch thick.

Cut into rounds. You can gently knead the scraps together to make a few more.

Place biscuits on a baking sheet. If you like soft sides, put them touching each other. If you like crusty sides, put them about 1 inch apart. The ones closer together will rise higher.

Bake 10 to 12 minutes, until light golden brown on top and bottom.

Serve with honey butter.

### Honey Butter

½ pound butter
2 tablespoons honey
½ teaspoon vanilla
¼ teaspoon cinnamon
Salt to taste

In a food processor or bowl, combine all ingredients and season lightly with salt.

> Tip: You can make these biscuits, cut them, and freeze them unbaked up to a month.

# Carrot Cookie Sandwiches with Honey Frosting

Makes 12 sandwiches

Preheat oven to 350°F.

1¼ cups flour

1 teaspoon cinnamon

1 teaspoon ground cloves

½ teaspoon baking powder

½ teaspoon salt

½ cup unsalted butter, room temperature

⅓ cup plus 2 tablespoons brown sugar, packed

⅓ cup plus 2 tablespoons granulated sugar

1 large egg

1 teaspoon vanilla

1 cup carrots, grated

2 teaspoons orange zest

Sift together flour, cinnamon, cloves, baking powder and salt; set aside.

In a large bowl, beat butter, sugars, egg, and vanilla until fluffy, about 2 minutes. Blend in carrots and zest. Add flour mixture until just combined.

Drop 1 tablespoon batter per cookie onto parchment-lined baking sheet. Bake cookies on center rack 14 to 16 minutes. Cool slightly on pan and transfer to wire racks.

## Honey Frosting

8 ounces Gina Marie cream cheese

3 tablespoons honey

½ cup walnuts or pecans, chopped

1 teaspoon orange zest

Blend all ingredients together.

To make sandwiches, put 1 tablespoon frosting between bottoms of 2 cookies. Voila! Sandwiches.

# *November 19*

# Spinach

Spinach, Fennel and Apple Salad with Champagne Vinaigrette
Salmon with Spinach and Pine Nuts
Spinach Ravioli with Winter Squash Cream

We know spinach is a good source of vitamin A and folic acid. It also contains oxalic acid. Cooking turns the oxalic acid into crystals that limit the absorption of iron but cooking also breaks down cell walls and allows us to take in more nutrients.

Fresh spinach salads make a hearty lunch or an elegant addition to dinner, but with a quick sauté, it makes an excellent side dish. When cooking spinach, we prefer to use grapeseed oil and a bit of garlic or onion, and cook it over high heat in a large pan. This prevents the spinach from stewing instead of sautéing.

You might be surprised to find honest-to-goodness dirt hiding inside stalks or between leafy greens the first time you bring home produce from the farmers market. It's a good thing. That dirt is an important reminder the produce has come directly from the field to you.

Everything on your plate, whether animal or vegetable, depends upon soil for life. Since you depend on food, your life is inextricably intertwined with the life of soil.

# Spinach

## Spinach, Fennel and Apple Salad with Champagne Vinaigrette

Serves 4

4 cups spinach leaves
1 medium fennel bulb, julienne
2 apples, cored and sliced
2 ounces goat cheese, crumbled
¼ cup pistachios

### Champagne Vinaigrette

3 tablespoon Champagne vinegar
1 lemon, juiced
¼ cup olive oil
Salt and pepper to taste

Combine salad ingredients. Whisk vinaigrette ingredients and toss with salad. Serve immediately.

*Drink the spinach water. The water in which vegetables are cooked is rich in vitamins and other healthful plant chemicals. Save it for soup or add it to sauces.*
   *—Michael Pollan.*

## Salmon with Spinach and Pine Nuts

Serves 6

3 cups spinach leaves, blanched
¼ cup Parmesan cheese
¼ cup sour cream
Salt and pepper to taste
2 tablespoons oil
2 to 3 pounds salmon, deboned and cut
   into 6 equal portions
¼ cup pine nuts, toasted

To blanch spinach, boil in salted water 30 to 45 seconds, then place in a bowl of ice water to cool. Drain completely and ring out excess water. Place spinach in a blender or food processor with Parmesan and sour cream. Purée until smooth. Season to taste with salt and pepper. Set aside. In a large sauté pan, heat oil. Season fish with salt and pepper, and sear on presentation side. When cooked ⅓ through, flip fish and turn off heat. Place 2 to 3 tablespoons spinach purée on each piece of fish and broil 2 to 3 minutes. Top with pine nuts before serving.

# Spinach Ravioli with Winter Squash Cream

## Pasta Dough

2 cups all purpose flour, plus more for dusting
1 teaspoon salt
3 eggs
2 tablespoons olive oil

To make pasta dough, combine flour and salt on a flat work surface; shape into a mound and make a well in the center. Add the eggs and olive oil to well and lightly beat with a fork. Gradually draw flour from inside the well wall in a circular motion. Use your hand for mixing, being careful to protect the outer wall. Continue to incorporate flour until it forms a ball. Sprinkle a dusting of flour on work surface, knead and fold dough until elastic and smooth, about 10 minutes. Wrap dough in plastic wrap; let rest for about 30 minutes to allow the gluten to relax.
To roll out, cut dough into 4 pieces and process through pasta machine, starting with the largest setting and working your way down, gradually making a thinner sheet with each pass. We used a hand-crank machine, and finished on setting 3. Place rolled sheets of pasta on a sheet tray lined with flour or cornmeal. Keep covered until ready to use.

## Filling

1 pound fresh spinach
1 pound ricotta cheese
1 egg
2 tablespoons heavy cream
¼ cup Parmesan cheese, grated
Salt and pepper to taste

Blanch spinach in a pot of boiling, salted water 30 to 45 seconds. Place in a bowl of ice water to cool. Drain completely and ring out excess moisture. Place on a paper towel to dry. Chop and place in a large bowl with ricotta, egg, cream and Parmesan. Season to taste with salt and pepper. Set aside.

## Winter Squash Cream

4 cups squash, peeled and cut in 2-inch pieces
2 cups half and half
2 tablespoons sage, chiffonade
Salt and pepper to taste

Cook squash in boiling, salted water until tender. Drain and place in a food processor with half and half. Purée until well blended. Stir in sage and season to taste with salt and pepper. Keep warm over low heat.

To assemble the ravioli, place 1 spoonful of filling onto 1 sheet of dough ½ inch from the edge. Continue to place spoonfuls of filling along the dough 1 inch from each other. Use your finger to run water along the edges and in between filling. Place 1 of the other pieces of rolled out dough on top of the piece with the filling on it. Pinch the dough around the filling to form the ravioli. Use a cookie cutter or a knife to cut out the ravioli. Pinch the edges of each ravioli with the tines of a fork. Set aside on a plate lightly dusted with flour. Do not stack, because they will stick together.
Cook raviolis in gently boiling, salted water until tender, 2 to 3 minutes, until they float. Drain and serve on a pool of cream, garnish with shaved Parmesan.

# Kale

Kale Chips

Chicken, Mushroom and Kale Soup

Sautéed Kale with Mushrooms and Onions

Sautéed Kale with Delicata Squash

Sautéed Kale with Taso Ham

## Kale Chips

*Thanks to Tina Gill for this recipe.*

1 cup red bell peppers, seeds removed
  and chopped

1 cup cashews

2 tablespoons nutritional yeast

2 to 4 tablespoons water

2 tablespoons agave syrup or honey

1 tablespoon olive oil

½ teaspoon salt

6 cups, or one bunch kale, leaves ripped into
  bite size pieces

Place all ingredients except kale in food processor. Blend into a thick cream, adding water until it's consistency of a creamy paste. Put kale pieces in a large bowl and pour the mixture over the kale. Mix with hands until the leaves are thoroughly coated.
Spread single layer of kale on dehydrator trays; dry at 104°F eight to 10 hours. Chips should be crispy.

# Kale

## Chicken, Mushroom & Kale Soup

Serves 4

½ cup dry orzo pasta
2 tablespoons olive oil
1 cup oyster mushrooms, diced
1 cup onion, diced
1 cup kale, stems removed
1 quart chicken stock
1 cup roasted chicken, shredded
Salt and pepper to taste

Heat 2 quarts water, add pasta, and cook on high heat until tender. Drain and set aside.
In a large pot, heat oil. Add mushrooms and sauté 2 minutes; add onions and sauté 2 minutes; add kale and stir until limp.
Pour in chicken stock and cook until hot.
Add chicken. Salt and pepper to taste; serve piping hot.
This soup is a great way to use leftover chicken.

## Sautéed Kale with Mushrooms and Onions

Serves 6

2 tablespoons butter
½ pound oyster mushrooms
1 clove garlic, minced
1 small onion, julienne
2 bunches kale, leaves torn into pieces
½ lemon, juiced
Salt and pepper to taste
Parmesan cheese, shaved, for garnish

Heat 1 tablespoon butter in a large sauté pan. Add mushrooms and cook until just caramelized. Add garlic and onions and season lightly with salt and pepper. Remove from pan; set aside. Add remaining butter to pan and sauté kale until wilted, about 1 minute. Add mushrooms back to pan; add lemon juice and season to taste with salt and pepper. Garnish individual servings with shaved Parmesan.

# Sautéed Kale with Delicata Squash

Serves 6

1 delicata squash
1 tablespoon butter
1 tablespoon olive oil
2 cloves garlic, chopped
2 bunches kale, leaves torn into pieces
3 tablespoons white wine
Salt and pepper to taste

To prepare squash, cut off one end and scoop out seeds as deep as you can reach. Slice squash ¼-inch thick on a mandolin. Remove any remaining seeds.
In a large sauté pan, heat butter and oil over medium heat. Add garlic and cook until fragrant. Add squash and sear on both sides, about 2 minutes. Remove from pan. Add kale leaves and wine to pan; sauté until leaves are wilted, about 1 minute. Add squash back to pan and season to taste with salt and pepper.

*Real dirt. Real food. Real health.*

# Sautéed Kale with Taso Ham

Serves 4

1 tablespoon butter
1 tablespoon olive oil
2 tablespoons red onions, diced
2 cloves garlic, chopped
3 to 4 ounces Taso ham, diced
2 bunches kale, leaves torn into pieces
Salt and pepper to taste

In a large sauté pan, heat butter and oil over medium high heat. Add onions, garlic and ham. Cook until ham begins to caramelize. Add kale leaves and sauté until leaves are wilted, about 1 minute. Add salt and pepper to taste.

# Garlic

Roasted Garlic

Sheep Camp Beans

Mushroom Potato Casserole

Seared Halibut with Garlic and Herb Compound Butter

Granny Moir's Scottish Shortbread

"Virtually everyone knows someone who has been diagnosed with cancer—which is not too surprising, since almost half of all American men and one-third of women will eventually develop cancer. Cancer is the second leading cause of death in the U.S., not far behind heart disease.

"There is good evidence that certain lifestyle changes can dramatically decrease the risk. Many experts, including the American Cancer Society, have come up with estimates similar to that of Richard Doll and Richard Peto who 30 years ago reported that smoking caused about 30% of all cancers in the U.S., and that poor diet and lack of physical activity (leading to excess body weight) were responsible for another 35%.

"This suggests that as many as two-thirds of all cancers, or about one million of the cancers diagnosed in 2011, might not have occurred if all Americans had quit (or never started) smoking, improved their diet and exercised more.

"What about the remaining 35%? About 10% are caused by genes that are inherited from a parent and increase cancer risk. Other cancers are linked to reproductive factors (like late childbearing), alcohol consumption or medical procedures that expose people to radiation. And still others-- though not as many as most people probably believe—are due to exposures to carcinogens and environmental toxins.

"For cancer prevention, the goal is to eat a healthy diet that contains lots of fruits, vegetables, beans and whole grains. If you do that, you are likely to decrease your intake of fat, especially animal fats. You'll also be more likely to stay at a healthy weight."

*Excerpted from the University of California, Berkeley "Wellness Letter" special supplement called "Preventing Cancer – Strategies that can reduce your risk." Written by John Swartzberg, MD, and Jeffrey Wolf, MD.*

# Garlic

## Roasted Garlic

Preheat oven to 400°F.

Serves 8

4 large heads garlic
2 tablespoons olive oil
Salt and pepper to taste
1 loaf artisan bread, cut into ¾-inch slices

Cut top half inch off garlic, exposing the cloves.
Remove excess skin. Place each head in a 6-inch
square piece of foil, drizzle with oil, salt and
pepper, and wrap edge up to top. Place in a
muffin tin and bake 30 to 40 minutes, until soft.
Serve with fresh bread.

# Sheep Camp Beans

Serves 6

*Thanks to Dan Macon of Flying Mule Farm for this recipe (in his words).*

1 pound chorizo

1 tablespoon olive oil

½ cup onions, diced

5 cloves garlic, diced

Red wine (not sure how much – pour until it looks good)

Water (same as above)

1 can pinto beans, drained

1 can kidney beans, drained

1 can stewed tomatoes, the Italian seasoned variety is best

1 can green chiles, diced

Dash of cinnamon

Salt and pepper to taste

Remove sausage from casings and brown in a Dutch oven. Remove from pot when done. Set aside.

Add olive oil to pot, and sauté onions and garlic. Add sausage, beans, wine, water and chiles. Season to taste. Cook low and slow several hours (all day, if possible). Have a taste of the red wine. Cook a bit longer. Serve with good bread!

> This recipe is best in a cast iron Dutch oven over a camp fire, but it can also be made in a crock pot. It changes each time I make it depending on what I have on hand.

# Mushroom Potato Casserole

Serves 6 to 8

Preheat oven to 375°F.

2 pounds potatoes, peeled

1 clove garlic

3 tablespoons butter

1 teaspoon salt

1 egg yolk, beaten

½ cup whole milk

½ pound small crimini mushrooms, sliced

2 teaspoons olive oil

⅓ cup Gruyère cheese, grated

⅓ cup Havarti cheese, grated

3 tablespoons fresh parsley, chopped

Boil potatoes and garlic until easily pierced with a fork. Drain potato water and, over low heat, slightly dry potatoes. Add butter and salt to pan; mash potatoes and garlic. Beat egg yolk with milk; add to potatoes. Set aside.

In a frying pan, sauté mushrooms with olive oil. Fold mushrooms, cheeses and parsley in potatoes. Pour potato mixture into buttered 1½-quart casserole dish. Cover and bake 30 minutes. Remove cover and bake 15 minutes longer to brown. Serve piping hot.

> Our choice for potatoes in this recipe is either German Butterball or Yukon Gold, but other potato varieties can be used. If making this casserole ahead, keep it unbaked and covered in the refrigerator, and return to room temperature before baking.
>
> When my children, now adults, come to visit, they request this mushroom potato casserole served with baked ham.

# Garlic

## Seared Halibut with Garlic and Herb Compound Butter

Serves 6

1 teaspoon olive oil
½ head red garlic, minced
¼ cup white wine
½ pound butter, room temperature
2 tablespoons parsley, chopped
1 tablespoon dill, chopped
1 Meyer lemon, zested
2 tablespoons grapeseed oil
2 to 3 pounds halibut
Salt and pepper to taste

To make garlic and herb compound butter, heat oil in a small sauté pan and cook garlic until fragrant over medium high heat. Add wine and continue cooking until reduced by about ⅔; remove from pan.

In a large mixing bowl, combine butter, herbs, lemon zest and garlic. Mix to combine and season to taste with salt and pepper.

On a 10-inch square piece of parchment paper, pile butter mixture across the center and bottom quarter of the paper, leaving a 3-inch border around the edge. Roll the butter in the paper, twist the sides to seal. Chill at least 1 hour before using.

In a large sauté pan, heat oil. Season fish with salt and pepper, and sear on presentation side until golden brown and cooked about ⅓ of the way through. Flip fish, top with 1 tablespoon compound butter, and turn off pan. Fish will continue to cook. Remove from pan when cooked to medium, or longer if desired.

# Granny Moir's Scottish Shortbread

Makes 2 dozen small squares

*Thanks to Barbara Read for this recipe from her grandmother. It makes a fine textured, traditional Scottish shortbread.*

Preheat oven to 350°F.

1¾ cups white flour
¼ cup rice flour (increase proportion of rice flour
    to white flour for a finer texture)
1 cup salted butter, softened
¾ cup sugar
¾ cup superfine (fruit) sugar

Blend flours. Set aside.

Blend together butter and sugars. Add flour mixture and blend until crumbly. Don't overwork. Press into a 9x9-inch pan. Pierce surface multiple times with fork before placing in oven.

Bake until golden brown, about 30 to 40 minutes. Remove from oven and cut into desired portion sizes. Shortbread will be soft. Let sit until it is firm enough to remove easily.

> ᕦᕤ Barbara's version: For a chewier, more crumbly texture, use 2 cups of white flour instead of white and rice flour, and 1 cup sugar (no superfine sugar).

*December 10*

# Citrus Medley

Citrus Salad

Orange Marmalade

Salmon Ceviche

Brussels Sprouts with Mandarins

I have an ant (versus grasshopper) mentality when it comes to food. I suppose it comes from growing up on a farm in Minnesota. Preserving vegetables like carrots, turnips, rutabagas and potatoes in our root cellar meant we'd eat well all winter. We also canned fruits and vegetables, and made jams, sauces, pickles and sauerkraut. To this day, I take great pleasure taking berries out of my freezer to enjoy on pancakes, oatmeal or as a dessert topping during the cold months. It's like having summer at my fingertips.

Although my interest in canning, drying and fermenting foods stems from childhood, I am fascinated by the rising interest in traditional food preservation techniques. Community centers across the country offer classes in canning and preserving. The number of "how to" books and internet resources have soared the last few years. This isn't a fad; it's a trend directly connected to the fresh, local seasonal food movement.

Canning, drying, fermenting and freezing are all inexpensive, sustainable ways to preserve Nature's bounty while maintaining control over what we eat.

# Citrus Medley

## Citrus Salad

Serves 4

6 oranges or mandarins (we used mandarins,
  Cara Cara and navel oranges), segmented
1 teaspoon olive oil
¼ cup pistachios

Combine all ingredients.
This salad is a perfect palate cleanser with a
hearty winter meal.

## Orange Marmalade

*Thanks to Dorothy Fields, Panajachel,
Guatemala, for this recipe.*

2 pounds oranges, mandarin oranges or
  kumquats, unpeeled, thinly sliced
1 large lemon, unpeeled, thinly sliced
9 cups cold water
8 cups sugar

Place fruit in a large saucepan. Cover with cold
water and let stand 24 hours.
Bring to a boil, add sugar and remove from heat.
Stir until sugar is dissolved. Let stand 24 hours.
Bring mixture to a boil again, and cook until jelly
test is firm. Allow at least 3 hours.
Place marmalade into hot, clean jelly jars and seal
tightly.

To test jam, jelly and marmalade for doneness: Put a small plate in the refrigerator for 15 minutes. Pour a spoonful of the hot jam, jelly or marmalade onto the plate and leave it in the fridge for five minutes. Push the edges of the marmalade with your finger; if it's wrinkly, it's set. Always test for setting point when the recipe suggests, if it isn't set, check every five minutes. Don't overcook. It's tempting to keep cooking to achieve a firmer set. A slightly looser marmalade is preferable to one that tastes scorched.

*Avoid foods that are pretending
to be something they are not.
—Michael Pollan*

ᴄᴇⅅ Ceviche can be made with almost any type of fresh seafood, but red snapper, sole, scallops and prawns are most popular. Start with fresh, quality seafood. The acid in the citrus "cooks" the fish, making it firmer and turning it opaque. Tomatoes, jalapenos and cilantro can be substituted for the capers and parsley to give this appetizer a Latin spin.

## Salmon Ceviche

Makes 2 cups

6 ounces salmon, deboned and small diced
1 teaspoon lime zest
¼ cup lime juice
½ cup orange juice
2 tablespoons capers, rinsed
½ red onion, minced
Salt and pepper to taste
1 tablespoon parsley, chopped

In a medium glass bowl, combine salmon, juice, capers and onions. Season lightly with salt and pepper and gently mix together. Cover and refrigerate 2 to 3 hours. Fish will begin to "cook" and become opaque. Stir in parsley and adjust seasoning if desired.
Serve with flatbread or tortilla chips.

## Brussels Sprouts with Mandarins

Serves 8

Preheat oven to 375°F.

1 cup mandarin juice
2 pounds Brussels sprouts, quartered
3 cloves garlic, minced
2 tablespoons olive oil
Salt and pepper to taste
6 mandarins, segmented

Over low heat, reduce mandarin juice to ¼ cup. Set aside.
In a large bowl, season Brussels sprouts with garlic, oil, salt and pepper. Roast on a sheet tray 15 to 25 minutes, until edges begin to brown. Toss immediately with mandarin juice and segments.

*www.theartofrealfood.com*

281

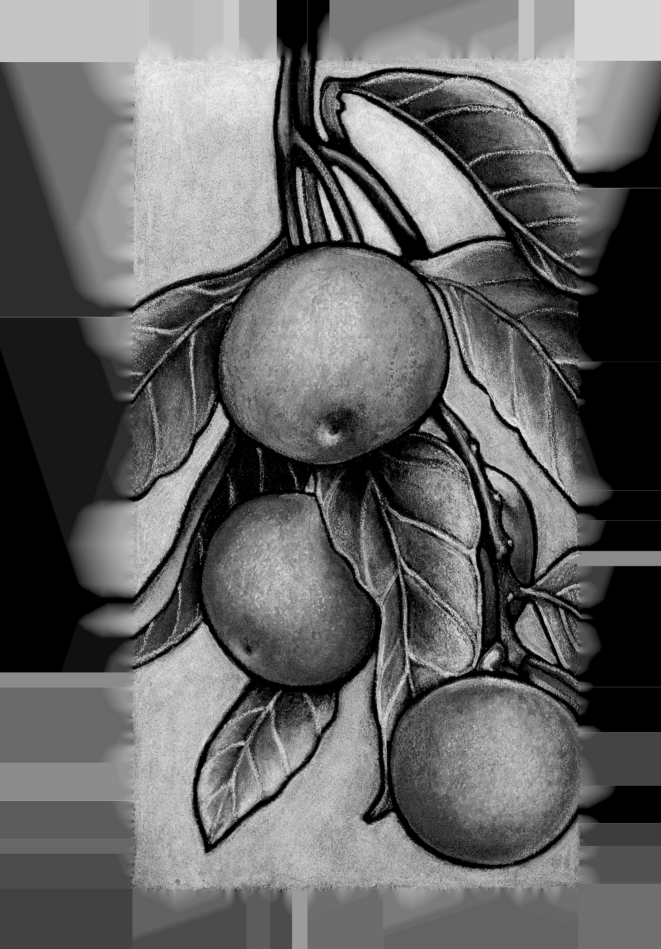

*December 17*

# Mandarins

Mulled Mandarin Juice

Fennel Slaw with Mandarin Vinaigrette

Mandarin and Fuyu Persimmon Salad

Prawn, Mandarin and Celery Stir Fry

Our garden is full of fruit trees: pomegranate, plum, persimmon, pear, fig, Meyer lemon, and Satsuma mandarin orange. We planted almost 50 mandarin trees 18 years ago, and they're mature enough to provide enough fruit for eating, juicing and sharing.

After mid-November we keep a watchful eye on the mandarins as they turn a gentle shade of orange. When the colors are right, we taste test for sweetness and flavor. Each mandarin must be carefully cut from the tree; the cut is made as close to the skin as possible. Pulling fruit off the twig tears the skin and fruits hold only a day or two. We store fruit in open-air containers because this allows the fruit to breathe.

Mandarins develop more intense flavors by being placed in a cool dry space for several days. They also keep well in an open container in the refrigerator. Last year our refrigerator held mandarins in good condition until late March.

Tests conducted by the USDA Albany Research Center show Placer County mandarins contain more than six times as much synephrine as other citrus. Synephrine is a decongestant. A decongestant is what we take to relieve symptoms of allergies and colds.

Give a child two or three easy-to-peel mandarins and watch the sniffles disappear. Remember to juice mandarins and freeze the juice to defrost and drink throughout the year. When allergy season shows up, drink an eight ounce glass of mandarin juice, and you'll feel better.

# Mandarins

## Mulled Mandarin Juice

Makes 6 cups

4 cups mandarin juice, freshly squeezed
  or frozen
2 cups unfiltered apple juice
1 mandarin peel, orange part cut into thin strips
3 cinnamon sticks, each 4 inches long
6 whole cloves
1 teaspoon ground allspice
6 whole green cardamom pods
½ teaspoon nutmeg
1 teaspoon fresh ginger, diced (optional)

Place all ingredients in a two-quart saucepan.
Bring to a boil and then immediately reduce heat
and simmer slowly 15 minutes. Taste. Add honey
for sweeter juice. Remove from heat and let juice
cool 1 hour. Strain and store in a jar in the
refrigerator. Serve cold, or, on a chilly night, hot,
garnished with a slice of mandarin.
Juice can be stored in refrigerator up to 3 days.

## Fennel Slaw with Mandarin Vinaigrette

Serves 4

2 cups fennel, shaved
Mint leaves for garnish

### Mandarin Vinaigrette

3 tablespoons mandarin juice
2 teaspoons shallots, diced
½ teaspoon Dijon mustard
1 teaspoon honey
1 tablespoon mint, chopped
¼ cup olive oil
Salt and pepper to taste

In a blender, purée mandarin juice, shallots,
mustard, honey and mint until combined. While
machine is running, add oil in a slow, steady
stream. Season to taste with salt and pepper.
Combine fennel with vinaigrette, and garnish
with mint leaves.

# Mandarin and Fuyu Persimmon Salad

Serves 4

5 mandarins, segmented
4 Fuyu persimmons, peeled and sliced
2 tablespoons pomegranate seeds
1 Asian pear, sliced

Combine all ingredients.

# Prawn, Mandarin and Celery Stir Fry

Serves 4

1 pound prawns, peeled and deveined
2 tablespoons mandarin juice
2 tablespoons grapeseed oil
2 cloves garlic, minced
½ onion, julienne
4 stalks celery, sliced
Salt and pepper to taste
½ cup celery leaves
1 teaspoon mandarin zest
¼ cup Snow's Citrus Court Mandarin Stir Fry Sauce
3 mandarins, segmented
¼ cup pistachios
2 cups brown rice, cooked
3 tablespoons scallions, sliced

In a medium bowl, combine prawns and mandarin juice. Cover and refrigerate up to 1 hour.

In a large sauté pan, heat 1 tablespoon oil, add garlic and onions and cook until fragrant. Add celery and continue to cook until just tender. Season lightly with salt and pepper, remove from pan. Set aside.

Heat remaining oil and add prawns and juice. Season lightly with salt and pepper and cook until almost opaque. Add onion and celery mixture, celery leaves, mandarin zest, and stir fry sauce. Toss to coat with mandarins and pistachios. Season to taste with salt and pepper. Serve over steamed brown rice and garnish with scallions.

# Sweet Potatoes

Sweet Potato and Lentil Soup

Sweet Potato Empanadas with Cilantro Ginger Dipping Sauce

Roasted Sweet Potatoes with Brown Sugar

Sweet Potato Hash with Ham

French Pastry

## Sweet Potato and Lentil Soup

Serves 6

*Thanks to Alia Shuttleworth for this recipe*

¼ cup butter

1 large sweet potato, peeled and chopped

2 large carrots, peeled and chopped

1 apple, cored and chopped

1 onion, chopped

½ cup red lentils

½ teaspoon ginger, minced

½ teaspoon black pepper

1 teaspoon salt

½ teaspoon ground cumin

½ teaspoon chili powder

½ teaspoon paprika

¼ teaspoon curry powder

Cayenne to taste

5 cups vegetable stock

Yogurt, for garnish

Melt butter in a large, heavy-bottomed pot over medium high heat. Add sweet potatoes, carrots, apple and onion; stir and cook until onions are translucent, about 10 minutes. Stir in lentils, spices and stock. Bring to a boil, reduce heat and simmer until lentils and vegetables are soft, about 30 minutes. Working in batches, carefully purée the soup in a blender, using a few quick pulses to start each time. Return soup to a clean pot and bring back to a simmer; add additional stock or water if needed to thin to desired consistency. Garnish with yogurt when serving.

# Sweet Potatoes

## Sweet Potato Empanadas with Cilantro Ginger Dipping Sauce

Serves 4 as an appetizer

*Thanks to Pam Wilson for this recipe.*

Preheat oven to 375°F.

1 large sweet potato
1 teaspoon ginger, grated
2 tablespoons scallions, sliced
Salt and pepper to taste
12 wonton wrappers
1 cup vegetable oil

Puncture sweet potato with a fork several times and roast 40 to 45 minutes, until soft. Cool slightly and scoop flesh into small bowl. Add ginger and scallions and stir to combine. Season to taste with salt and pepper.

Place about 1 teaspoon of potato mixture in the center of each wonton wrapper. Using water to seal the inside edges, fold over to create a triangle pouch. Place in a single layer on a sheet tray lined with parchment paper.

In a medium pot, heat oil to 350°F. Fry empanadas a few at a time, until golden brown and crispy. Remove from oil and set on paper towels to drain. Can be reheated in a 350°F oven. Serve warm with cilantro ginger dipping sauce.

*Make water your beverage of choice.*
*—Michael Pollan*

## Cilantro Ginger Dipping Sauce

½ cup mayonnaise
½ cup sour cream
3 tablespoons ginger, grated
4 cloves garlic, minced
¼ cup cilantro, chopped
1 to 2 tablespoons Tamari soy sauce, to taste
Wasabi paste to taste
Salt and pepper to taste

Combine all ingredients and season to taste with wasabi, salt and pepper.

> ⤸ Tamari soy sauce is a darker form of soy sauce. It is still made from fermented soy beans and wheat, but the ratios are different and the result is a darker, richer soy sauce. For this particular recipe, using tamari makes a difference.

## Roasted Sweet Potatoes with Brown Sugar

Serves 8

Preheat oven to 375°F.

3 tablespoons butter, melted
3 tablespoons brown sugar
5 large sweet potatoes, peeled and cut into 1-inch pieces
1 teaspoon rosemary, finely diced
Salt and pepper to taste
3 mandarins, sectioned (optional)

Combine butter and sugar and toss with sweet potatoes. Season with rosemary, salt and pepper. Roast on a sheet tray 20 to 25 minutes, until tender. Garnish with mandarins before serving.

# Sweet Potato Hash with Ham

Serves 4

1 tablespoon olive oil
3 tablespoons butter
2 pounds sweet potatoes, peeled and diced
1 onion, diced
1 green bell pepper, diced
1 cup ham, cubed
2 teaspoons thyme
2 teaspoons oregano
Salt and pepper to taste
4 eggs, fried

Heat oil and 2 tablespoons butter in a large skillet and add potatoes. Cook over medium heat until slightly browned and tender. Add onions and bell peppers and continue cooking until softened. Remove from pan and set aside.
Heat remaining tablespoon butter over high heat and sauté ham until caramelized. Add potato mixture back to pan and caramelize all together. Season with herbs, salt and pepper. Garnish with fried egg.

# French Pastry

Makes 3 dozen small squares

Preheat oven to 350°F.

1 cup plus 2 tablespoons all purpose flour
½ cup butter, room temperature
¼ cup sugar
2 eggs, well beaten
1 teaspoon baking powder
1½ cups brown sugar
1½ teaspoons vanilla
¾ cup walnuts, chopped
1 cup coconut

Blend 1 cup flour, butter and sugar together using a pastry blender or a fork. Place blended dough in 7x13-inch baking pan and pat firmly. Pierce surface multiple times with a fork. Bake 10 minutes.
While pastry is baking, mix together eggs, remaining flour, baking powder, brown sugar and vanilla. Fold in walnuts and coconut. Spread mixture over baked layer and bake an additional 20 to 30 minutes.
Cool and cut in 1½-inch squares. Refrigerate.

*December 31*

# Pomegranates

Pomegranate Cocktails
Pomegranate Salsa
Flank Steak Marinade
Rack of Lamb with Mandarin–Pomegranate Syrup

## Pomegranate Cocktail

Serves 4...maybe

1 bottle sparkling wine
2 tablespoons pomegranate juice
2 tablespoons pomegranate seeds

Pour wine in glasses, ⅔ full. Add juice and seeds; enjoy.

There is always an occasion for bubbles. In the summer, we like to add a splash of peach or plum nectar. Mandarins and berries are fun additions as well.

# Pomegranates

## Pomegranate Salsa

Serves 4

1½ cups pomegranate seeds
2 limes, juiced
2 tablespoons mint, chiffonade
2 teaspoons olive oil
Salt and pepper to taste

Combine all ingredients and season to taste with salt and pepper. This is a wonderful accompaniment to roasted chicken or fish.

## Flank Steak Marinade

Serves 6 to 8

Heat grill.

½ cup olive oil
½ cup pomegranate balsamic vinegar
½ cup red wine vinegar
2 tablespoons soy sauce
2 tablespoons Worcestershire sauce
¼ cup brown sugar, firmly packed
1 tablespoon fresh rosemary, chopped
Salt and pepper to taste
2 cloves garlic, finely diced (optional)
2 pounds flank steak

To make marinade: Combine olive oil, vinegars, soy sauce, Worcestershire sauce, sugar, rosemary, salt and pepper. Blend well.
Place flank steak in a Pyrex pan and cover with marinade. Marinate 2 hours. Turn steak at least once.
Heat grill to very hot. Grill grass-fed steak no more than 2 minutes each side. Remove meat from grill and let it rest 5 minutes. Diagonally slice meat into thin pieces.
Leftover meat makes tasty sandwiches, and is great in a stir fry.

# Rack of Lamb with Mandarin-Pomegranate Syrup

Serves 4

*Thanks to Dan Macon of Flying Mule Farm for this grass-fed lamb recipe.*

Heat grill.

## Paste

2 tablespoons extra virgin olive oil
1 tablespoon garlic, minced
1 tablespoon Spanish paprika
2 teaspoons kosher salt
1 teaspoon freshly ground black pepper
2 racks lamb

## Syrup

1 cup fresh mandarin juice
1 cup pomegranate juice
2 tablespoons honey
1 tablespoon balsamic vinegar
1 teaspoon kosher salt

In a small bowl, mix paste ingredients. Spread over dry lamb racks. Set aside to stand at room temperature for 20 to 30 minutes before grilling. In a small saucepan, combine mandarin juice, pomegranate juice, honey and balsamic vinegar. Bring to a boil over high heat. Once boiling, reduce heat to medium and simmer until liquid is reduced to ⅓ cup (15 to 20 minutes). Season syrup with salt and let cool. Syrup can be refrigerated up to 3 days.

Grill lamb over medium heat, bone sides down. Keep lid closed as much as possible. Continue cooking to desired doneness (13 to 18 minutes) for medium rare. Turn lamb once or twice and move racks over indirect heat if flare-up occurs. Remove lamb from grill and let rest 5 minutes before carving into chops.

Warm syrup over low heat until it reaches desired consistency. Drizzle over warm lamb.

Some plants, including many fruit trees and herbs, benefit from being a bit stressed. Our property provides that stress naturally: our thin soil is filled with stones, and we have a limited amount of water. Once we recognized our property should be called Gardenstone, we chose fruit trees that thrive in stressed soil. Pomegranate, olive, and persimmon trees are in this category. In fact, if persimmon trees are over-watered, there will be little or no fruit.

Trees like mandarin, Meyer lemon and kumquat trees like to be a little thirsty when fruit is ripening. Four to six weeks before picking, we decrease the amount of irrigation given the citrus trees. In addition, once picked, we place citrus into a cool dry place for at least three or four days before eating. We have some of the best citrus around: fruit that is fully colored, juicy and full of flavor.

*Comments by Michael Pollan are taken from his book, "Food Rules, an Eater's Manual." (The Penguin Press, New York, 2011, 211 pages).*

*Real dirt. Real food. Real Health.*

## A

**APPETIZERS**
ahi poke cucumber boats, 166
baba ganoush, 240
baked cherries with taleggio cheese, 135
blue cheese stuffed tomatoes, 203
fried green tomatoes, 218
fried padron peppers, 223
grilled grapes with brie cheese, 211
halibut croquettes with tartar sauce, 212
kale chips, 269
persimmon dip, 234
roasted garlic, 274
salmon ceviche, 281
smoked salmon spread with sliced cucumbers, 166
spiced nuts, 28
sweet potato empanadas, 288
walnut crostini with ricotta cheese and cherries, 134

**APPLES**
about, 231
apple juice baked beans, 141
cake, 229
galette, 230
mulled mandarin juice, 284
pie, 231
sauce, 228
sautéed, 229
salad, with fennel and spinach, 266
soup, with fennel, 50
with quinoa, 228
with roasted delicata squash  and walnuts, 254
vinaigrette, 245

**APRICOTS**
chutney, 108

**ARUGULA**
blue cheese burgers, 146
flatbread with blue cheese and figs, 160
leg of lamb, 147
pasta, with chili flakes, 145
pizza, about, 145

**ARTICHOKES**
with balsamic reduction, 196

**ASPARAGUS**
amaranth cakes, 87
chicken wraps with lemon and herbs, 107
with pasta, mushrooms, spring onions, 119

## B

**BACON**
with braised endives, 59
with fennel and apple soup, 50
with flatbread, figs and blue cheese, 160
with mac n'cheese, 128
with potatoes, 118
vinaigrette, 72

**BAHARAT**
about, 28, 185
carrot soup, 94
quinoa and corn cakes, 185
spice, 185

spiced croutons, 94
spiced nuts, 28

**BARLEY**
scotch broth, 259
soup, with mushrooms , 89

**BEANS, DRIED**
about, 139
baked, 141
baked with apple juice, 141
flageolet with lamb, 147
flageolet with pork tenderloin, 121
sheep camp, 275
soup with cannellini beans, celery and ham, 258
soup with lamb and white beans, 140
stew with black beans and sausage, 140

**BEANS, FRESH**
about, 200
grilled romano beans with prosciutto, 200
salad, niçoise, 199
salad, potato and green bean, 75
sautéed snake beans, 200
stir fry with beef and tomatoes 204
succotash, 196
with roasted chicken, tomatoes and mushrooms, 205

**BEEF**
brisket with persimmon glaze, 236
burgers, blue cheese, 146
chicken fried steak with mashed potatoes, 77
flank steak marinade, 292
flank steak with root vegetables, 40
pasties, 41
ribs with barbecue sauce, 174
roast beef and bok choy, 69
sauce, spaghetti with wild meat, 221
short ribs, braised, 97
short ribs, tomato braised, 175
stew, red wine, 95
stir fry with tomatoes, 204

**BEETS**
chocolate cake, 73
pickled, 72
salad, roasted with bacon vinaigrette, 72
salad, roasted with cucumbers, 71
salad, with fennel and oranges, 50

**BERRIES** (see blackberries, blueberries, raspberries, strawberries)
about, 115, 123, 127, 187, 188

**BISCUITS**
buttermilk with honey butter, 262

**BLACKBERRIES**
about, 123, 127, 187, 188
cobbler, with rhubarb, 188
crisp, 192
dessert crepes with nectarines, 157
galette, with pear, 190
galette, with plum, 191
galette, with rhubarb, 189
pie, with nectarines, 156
vinaigrette, 188

**BLUEBERRIES**
about, 123
cake, kuchen, 130
cake, tea with lemon, 131
pie, with nectarines, 155

**BROCCOLI**
about, 33
frittata, 225
soup, with cheese, 34
with quinoa and turkey, 37

**BRUSSELS SPROUTS**
with mandarins, 281

**C**

**CABBAGE**
about sauerkraut, 65
bok choy, with roast beef, 69
brisket, with persimmon glaze, 236
sauerkraut, with pork chops and mashed potatoes, 68
sausage wrapped in cabbage leaves, 67
spicy jicama slaw, 66

**CAKE**
angel food,
        about, 25, 163
        cake, 24, 30, 162
         rocky road cake, 162, 163
         4th of July cake, 162, 163
        with Meyer lemon sauce, 24
        with walnuts and pistachios, 30
apple, 229
Asian pear, 249
blueberry kuchen, 130
cheesecake, 193
cheesecake, mini, 129
chocolate beet, 73
chocolate ganache, 201
double lemon, 23
lemon and blueberry, 131
persimmon loaf, 237
pistachio, 31
pound, polenta, 91
raisin and nut, 215

**CARROTS**
about, 93
beer braised rabbit, 96
braised short ribs, 97
cookie sandwiches, 263
soup with baharat-spiced croutons, 94
stew, red wine, 95

**CAULIFLOWER**
about, 45
roasted, with lemon and pine nuts, 47
soup, 46
steamed, with cheese sauce, 46

**CELERY**
about, 257
bloody Mary, 258
scotch broth, 259
soup, with heirloom cannellini beans and ham, 258
stir fry, with prawns and mandarins, 285

**CELERY ROOT**
about, 259
purée, 259

**CHAMPAGNE**
vinaigrette, 266

**CHARD** (see Swiss chard)

**CHERRIES**
about, 133
baked, with taleggio cheese, 135
pie, 137
sauce, with balsamic vinegar, 136
topping, with apricots, 135
with walnut crostini and ricotta cheese, 134

**CHICKEN**
about, 204
crepes, 120
livers, with balsamic vinegar and goat cheese, 82
roasted, with fennel and snap peas, 51
roasted, with rosemary, 109
roasted, with tomatoes, green beans and mushrooms, 205
soup, with mushrooms and kale, 270
with green tomatoes and tarragon, 220
with mandarin mustard glaze and romanesco, 36
wraps, with asparagus, lemon and herbs, 107
wraps, with walnuts and cranberries, 28

**CHOCOLATE**
about, 73, 201
beet cake, 73
brownies, 248
ganache cake, 201

**CHUTNEY**
apricot, 108
persimmon, 234

**COBBLER**
blackberry and rhubarb, 188

**COOKIES**
carrot, 263
pistachio meringue, 29
shortbread, 277

**CORN**
about, 183
cakes, with quinoa, 185
relish, with cherry tomatoes, 184
salsa, with roasted peppers and tomatoes, 217
sauce, with jalapeno, 184
succotash, 196
tortillas, 183

**CORNSTARCH SLURRY,** 63

**COUS COUS**
with mushrooms, 90

**CRANBERRIES**
sauce, 236
walnut wraps, 28

**CREPES**
dessert with nectarines and blackberries, 157
savory, with chicken, 120

**CROSTINI**
blue cheese, with mushroom soup, 86
walnut, with ricotta cheese and cherries, 134
with smoked salmon and hard boiled eggs, 100

**CRUCIFEROUS VEGETABLES**
About, 33
**CUCUMBERS**
ahi poke cucumber boats, 166
kosher dill pickles, 168
pickle relish, 224
salad, polenta panzanella, 208
salad, with roasted beets, 71
with shrimp soup, 167
with smoked salmon spread, 166

# D
**DESSERT**
angel food cake, 4th of July, 162, 163
angel food cake, rocky road, 162, 163
angel food cake, with Meyer lemon sauce, 24
angel food cake, with walnuts or pistachios, 30
apple cake, 229
apple galette, 230
apple pie full of flavor, 231
apples, sautéed, 229
applesauce, 228
Asian pear cake, 249
Asian pear pie, 249
blackberry and pear galette, 190
blackberry and plum galette, 191
blackberry and rhubarb cobbler, 188
blackberry and rhubarb galette, 189
blackberry crisp, 192
brownies, 248
butterscotch sauce, 29
carrot cookie sandwiches, 263
cheesecake, 193
cheesecake, mini, 129
cherry pie, 137
chocolate beet cake, 73
chocolate ganache cake, 201
crepes, 157
double lemon cake, 23
Finnish pancakes, 124
French pastry, 289
fruit pops, 179
lemon and blueberry tea cake, 131
Meyer lemon shaum torte, 22
Meyer lemon sour pudding, 21
nectarine and blackberry pie, 156
nectarine and blueberry pie, 155
nectarine galette, 154
nectarines with honey and almonds, 153
peach and raspberry galette, 180
peach tart tatin, 181
pear crumble, 248
persimmon loaf, 237
pistachio cake, 31
pistachio ice cream balls, 209
pistachio meringue cookies, 29
plum and ground cherry pie, 175
polenta pound cake, 91
pumpkin pie, 255
pumpkin pie, heirloom with walnut crust, 255
raisin and nut cake, 215
rhubarb and raspberry pie, 115
Scottish shortbread, 277
strawberry fruit fool, 125
strawberry rhubarb sauce, 125
tapioca cream pudding, with sheep's milk, 103
**DRESSING** (see also vinaigrette)
lime ancho, 66
**DRINKS**
bloody Mary, 258
mojitos, 106
mulled mandarin juice, 284
pomegranate cocktails, 291

# E
**EGGPLANT**
baba ganoush 240
sandwich, grilled, 242
with quinoa, 241
**EGGS**
about, 99, 102
fried, with sweet potato hash, 289
frittata, with broccoli and peppers, 225
hard boiled, with crostini and smoked salmon, 100
salad, niçoise, 199
salad, potato, 101
sandwich, croque madam, 102
sandwich, egg salad, 100
**ENDIVE**
braised, 59
jambon, 58
salad, with fennel, 56
salad, with oranges, 62
salad, with pine nuts, 56
with pork chops, 57

# F
**FENNEL**
about, 49
lasagna, with Dungeness crab, 52
pasta with tomatoes and peppers, 204
roast beef, with fennel pollen, 69
salad, with beets and oranges, 50
salad, with endive, 56
salad, with spinach and apples, 266
slaw, with mandarin vinaigrette, 284
soup, with apples, 50
with roasted chicken and snap peas, 51
with sand dabs and pink rice, 51
**FERMENTED FOODS**
about, 165
about, pickled herring, 76
kosher dill pickles, 168
**FIGS**
candied dried, 159
salad, 161
with flatbread and blue cheese, 160
with yogurt and Asian pears, 247
**FISH** (see also seafood)
cod
miso crusted, 209

halibut
cheeks, with pink-eyed peas, 197
croquettes, 212
seared, with garlic and herb compound butter, 276
seared, with tomato peach salsa, 178
pickled herring
about, 76
with mashed potatoes and onions, 76
salmon
cakes, with Meyer lemon relish, 20
ceviche, 281
seared, with celery root purée, 259
seared, with grape salsa, 213
seared, with oranges, 63
smoked salmon spread, with sliced cucumbers, 166
smoked, with crostini and hard boiled eggs, 100
with spinach and pine nuts, 266
sand dabs, with pink rice, 51
tuna
ahi poke cucumber boats, 166
niçoise salad, 199

**G**

**GALETTE**
apple, 230
blackberry and pear, 190
blackberry and plum, 191
blackberry and rhubarb, 189
dough, 189
nectarine, 154
peach and raspberry, 180
**GARLIC**
compound butter, 276
mushroom potato casserole, 275
roasted, 274
sheep camp beans, 275
**GINGER**
chips, with pear sauce, 247
reduction, with spicy anise, 47
sauce, with cilantro, 288
vinaigrette with honey, 161
**GRAINS**
amaranth cakes, with mushrooms, 87
barley, soup with mushrooms, 89
cous cous, with mushrooms, 90
grits, with prawns, 91
polenta pound cake, 91
quinoa corn cakes, 185
quinoa, autumn, 228
quinoa, Greek style salad, 241
quinoa, with pears, 246
quinoa, with turkey and broccoli, 37
quinoa, stuffed tomatoes, 151
rice, green, 109
rice, pink, 51
salad, polenta panzanella, 208
scotch broth, 259
**GRAPES**
grilled, with brie cheese, 211
raisin and nut cake, 215

salsa, 213
with pork chops and blue cheese, 214
**GREEN BEANS** (see beans, fresh)
**GRITS**
with prawns, 91
**GROUND CHERRIES**
about, 172
pie, with plums, 175
pork tenderloin, 173
salsa, 172

**H**

**HALIBUT** (see fish)
**HERBS**
about, 105
chicken wraps with asparagus and lemon, 107
garlic compound butter, 276
green rice, 109
green tomato and tarragon chicken, 220
lemon dill sauce, 185
mint mojitos, 106
pink eyed peas with halibut cheeks, 197
rosemary roasted chicken, 109
**HONEY**
about, 261
butter, 262
frosting, 263
ginger honey vinaigrette, 161
mandarin pomegranate syrup, 293
St. Nick melon salad, 261
with citrus roasted rabbit, 62
with nectarines and almonds, 153

**J**

**JERUSALEM ARTICHOKES**
about, 34
soup, 34
**JICAMA**
spicy slaw, 66

**K**

**KALE**
chips, 269
sautéed with delicata squash, 271
sautéed with mushrooms and onions, 270
sautéed with taso ham, 271
soup with chicken and mushrooms, 270
**KOHLRABI**
about, 82
with lettuce wraps, 83
with mixed greens and radishes, 82

**L**

**LAMB**
chops, with peppers, 225
leg of lamb, arugula crusted, 147
rack, with mandarin pomegranate syrup, 293
scotch broth, 259
soup, with white beans, 140
stew, with black beans and spicy sausage, 140
**LASAGNA**
with crab, fennel and mushrooms, 52
**LEEKS**
soup, with Jerusalem artichokes and potatoes, 34

with butternut squash and mushroom casserole, 253

**LEFTOVERS**
about, 17, 35, 85, 118, 212
mashed potatoes, 76
stacked potatoes and onions, 118

**LEMONS, EUREKA**
cake, double lemon , 23
chicken wraps with asparagus and herbs, 107

**LEMONS, MEYER**
about, 19
cake, 23
icing, cream cheese, 163
relish, with salmon cakes, 20
sauce, lemon dill, 185
sauce, lemon sabayon, 25
shaum torte, 22
sour pudding, 21
tea cake, with blueberries, 131
vinaigrette with mandarins, 56

**LETTUCE**
mixed greens with chicken livers and goat cheese, 82
mixed greens with kohlrabi and radishes, 82
with roasted beets and bacon, 72
with strawberries, 125
wraps, 83

**M**

**MANDARINS**
about, 283
chicken, with romanesco, 36
citrus salad, 280
mandarin pomegranate syrup, 293
mulled mandarin juice, 284
reduction, 42
root vegetables, with mandarin reduction, 42
salad, with Fuyu persimmons, 285
stir fry, with prawns and celery, 285
vinaigrette, 284
with Brussels sprouts, 281

**MELONS**
ice cream balls, with pistachios, 209
salad, mixed melon, 207
salad, polenta panzanella, 208
salad, St. Nick, 261

**MEYER LEMON** (see lemons, Meyer)

**MUSHROOMS**
about, 87
arancini, 85
casserole, with butternut squash, 253
casserole, with potatoes, 275
lasagna with Dungeness crab, 52
pasta, with asparagus and spring onions, 119
purée, 86
soup, 86
soup, with barley, 89
soup, with chicken and kale, 270
with amaranth cakes, 87
with cous cous, 90
with roasted chicken, tomatoes, and green beans, 205

**N**

**NECTARINES**
about, 153
galette, 154
pie, with blackberries, 156
pie, with blueberries, 155
with crepes, 157
with honey and almonds, 153

**NUTS**
about, 27
angel food cake with walnuts or pistachios, 30
autumn apple cake, 229
autumn raisin and nut cake, 215
butternut squash salad, 252
chicken, cranberry and walnut wraps, 28
citrus salad with pistachios, 280
endive salad with pine nuts, 56
French pastry, 289
honey frosting, 263
pistachio cake, 31
pistachio ice cream balls, 209
pistachio meringue cookies, 29
roasted delicata squash with apples and walnuts, 254
rocky road cake, 162, 163
salmon with spinach and pine nuts, 266
spiced nuts, 28
St. Nick melon with honey and walnuts, 261
walnut crust, 255

**O**

**OLIVE OIL**
about, 81

**ONIONS**
about, 117
balsamic, with chicken livers and goat cheese, 82
pasta, with spring onions, 119
Placer Sweet onions and stacked potatoes, 118
with pickled herring and mashed potatoes, 76
with pork tenderloin and flageolet beans, 121

**ORANGES**
citrus roasted rabbit, 62
marmalade, 280
salad, citrus, 280
salad, with beets and fennel, 50
salad, with chipotle vinaigrette, 62
salad, with endive, 62
with arugula crusted leg of lamb, 147
with seared salmon, 63

**P**

**PANCAKES**
Finnish, 124

**PARSNIPS** (see root vegetables)
about, 39

**PASTA**
about, 96
basic pasta recipe, 53
lasagna with Dungeness crab, 52
mac n cheese, 128
spaghetti sauce, 221
spinach ravioli, 267

with arugula and chili flakes, 145
with asparagus, mushrooms and spring onions, 119
with braised rabbit and baby carrots, 96
with chicken, mushroom and kale soup, 270
with tomato braised short ribs, 175
with tomatoes, fennel and peppers, 204

**PASTIES**, 41

**PEACHES**
about, 177, 180
fruit pops, 179
galette, with raspberries, 180
salsa, with tomatoes, 178
tart tatin, 181
with roast pork, 179

**PEARS**
cake, 249
crumble, 248
galette, with blackberries, 190
pie, 249
salad, with apple juice vinaigrette, 245
sauce, with ginger chips, 247
with figs and yogurt, 247
with quinoa, 246

**PEPPERS**
about, padron, 223
about, roasted, 217
fried padron, 223
frittata with broccoli, 225
pasta, with tomatoes and fennel, 204
pickle relish, 224
salsa with roasted tomatoes, 217
sauce, with corn and jalapeno, 184
with lamb chops, 225
with steamed mussels, 224

**PERSIMMONS**
about, 234, 236
chutney, 234
dip, 234
glaze, 236
loaf, 237
salad, grilled, 235
salad, with mandarins, 285
sauce, cranberry, 236

**PIE**
apple, 231
Asian pear, 249
blackberry and rhubarb cobbler, 188
cherry, 137
nectarine and blackberry, 156
nectarine and blueberry, 155
pear crumble, 248
plum and ground cherry, 175
pumpkin (or squash), 255
pumpkin, heirloom, 255
rhubarb and raspberry, 115

**PIE CRUST**
about, 137
basic, 115
walnut, 255

**PINK-EYED PEAS**
about, 195
herbed with halibut cheeks, 197
succotash, 196

**PIZZA**
dough, whole wheat, 144
grilled, 144
sauce, herb garden pesto, 145
sauce, tomato, 144

**POLENTA**
panzanella salad, 208
pound cake, 91

**POMEGRANATES**
cocktail, 291
flank steak marinade, 292
salad, with grilled persimmon, 235
salsa, 292
syrup, with mandarins, 293
with persimmon chutney, 234
with quinoa and pears, 246

**PORK**
chili verde, 219
chops, with cherry balsamic sauce, 136
chops, with endive, 57
chops, with grapes and blue cheese, 214
chops, with sauerkraut and mashed potatoes, 68
endive jambon, 58
grilled Romano beans with prosciutto, 200
meatballs, with apricot chutney, 108
ribs, with mustard barbecue sauce, 243
roasted, with peaches, 179
sausage wrapped in cabbage leaves, 67
sautéed kale with taso ham, 271
sheep camp beans with chorizo, 275
soup, with cannellini beans, celery and ham, 258
sweet potato hash with ham, 289
tenderloin, with ground cherries, 173
tenderloin, with Placer Sweet onions and flageolet beans, 121

**POTATOES**
about, au gratin, 78
au gratin, 78
baked, stuffed with romanesco, 79
casserole, with mushrooms, 275
mashed, with pickled herring, 76
mashed, with roasted romanesco, 76
mashed, stacked with Placer Sweet onions, 118
mashed, with chicken fried steak, 77
mashed, with pork chops and sauerkraut, 68
pasties, 41
salad, 101
salad, with green beans, 75
soup, with Jerusalem artichokes and leeks, 34

**POULTRY,** see chicken or turkey

**PUDDING**
Meyer lemon, 21
sheep's milk tapioca, 103

**Q**

**QUINOA**
autumn, 228
corn cakes, 185

salad, Greek style, 241
squash stuffed tomatoes, 151
with pears, 246
with turkey and broccoli, 37

## R

**RABBIT**
beer braised, 96
citrus roasted, 62

**RAISINS**
cake, 215
persimmon loaf, 237

**RASPBERRIES**
about, 123
galette, with peaches, 180
pie, with rhubarb, 115

**RAVIOLI**
dough, 267
with spinach and winter squash cream, 267

**REDUCTIONS**
balsamic, 82, 196
mandarin, 42
spicy anise and ginger, 47

**RELISH**
cherry and apricot, 135
corn and cherry tomato, 184
Meyer lemon, 20
pickle, 224

**RHUBARB**
cobbler, with blackberries, 188
galette, with blackberries, 189
pie, with raspberries, 115
sauce with strawberries, 125

**RICE**
green, 109
mushroom arancini, 85
pink, with sand dabs, 51

**ROMANESCO**
roasted, with potato mash, 76
with mandarin chicken, 36
with baked potatoes, 79

**ROMANO BEANS** (see beans, fresh)
grilled, 200
salad, niçoise, 199
succotash, 196

**RUTABAGA** (see root vegetables)
about, 39

**ROOT VEGETABLES** (rutabagas, turnips, parsnips)
about, 39
roasted, with mandarin reduction, 42
rutabaga with love, 43
with flank steak, 40

## S

**SALADS**
butternut squash, 252
chicken livers with goat cheese, 82
citrus, 280
endive and orange, 62
endive with fennel, 56
endive with pine nuts, 56
fennel slaw, 284
fennel, beet and orange, 50
figs with ginger honey vinaigrette, 161
Greek style with quinoa, 241
green leaf with strawberries, 125
grilled persimmon, 235
mixed greens with kohlrabi and radishes, 82
mixed melon, 207
niçoise, 199
orange with chipotle vinaigrette, 62
pear with apple juice vinaigrette, 245
polenta panzanella, 208
potato, 101
potato and green bean, 75
roasted beets with bacon, 72
roasted beets with cucumbers, 71
romaine with blackberry vinaigrette, 188
spicy jicama slaw, 66
spinach, apple and fennel, 266
St. Nick melon, 261

**SALMON** (see fish)

**SALSA**
grape, 213
ground cherry, 172
jerry's tomato, 172
pomegranate, 292
roasted pepper and tomato, 217
tomato peach, 178

**SANDWICH**
brisket with persimmon glaze, 236
croque madam, 102
egg salad, 100
grilled eggplant, 242

**SAUCE**
apple, 228
blue cheese love, 113
butterscotch, 29
cherry balsamic, 136
cilantro ginger, 288
classic barbecue, 174
corn and jalapeno, 184
cranberry, 236
herb garden pesto, 145
lemon dill, 185
Meyer lemon sabayon, 25
mustard barbecue, 243
pear with ginger chips, 247
roasted red pepper aioli, 218
spaghetti, 221
strawberry rhubarb, 125
sun dried tomato aioli, 242
tartar, 212
tomato, 144

**SAUERKRAUT**
about, 65
with pork chops and mashed potatoes, 68

**SEAFOOD** (see also fish)
grits with prawns, 91
lasagna with Dungeness crab, 52
prawn mandarin and celery stir fry, 285